LIVE YOUR
LIFE'S PURPOSE

Also by the author

The Purpose of Love

LIVE YOUR
LIFE'S PURPOSE

A guidebook for creating and living a Purposeful Life

DOROTHY RATUSNY

INSOMNIAC PRESS

Library and Archives Canada Cataloguing in Publication

Ratusny, Dorothy
    Live your life's purpose : a guidebook for creating and living a purposeful life / Dorothy Ratusny.

ISBN 978-1-897178-68-3

1. Self-actualization (Psychology). 2. Happiness. 3. Self-esteem. 4. Consciousness. I. Title.

BF637.S4R382 2008   158.1   C2008-904294-8

The publisher gratefully acknowledges the support of the Department of Canadian Heritage through the Book Publishing Industry Development Program.

Printed and bound in Canada

Insomniac Press
192 Spadina Avenue, Suite 403
Toronto, Ontario, Canada, M5T 2C2
www.insomniacpress.com

Canada

For my mother,
who taught me how to read and write before I was
even old enough to attend school. Unknowingly, she
gave me what have become two of my most treasured
gifts. For this I am eternally grateful.

TABLE OF CONTENTS

ACKNOWLEDGMENTS

I am truly grateful for the many gifts that I have been blessed with and for the ability to continually hone these gifts. I acknowledge that I have been given a very special life's purpose, which I make an effort to live consciously—and on a daily basis. Knowing my life's purpose allows me to be responsible to it, as I share who I am with others.

I first understood the meaning of destiny most clearly more than a decade ago when I met Ryan. His capacity for giving me unconditional love has made it possible for me to grown and evolve in incredible ways, both in spirit and as a human being. Knowing that we are together in one more lifetime gives me the strength to create infinite possibilities.

My parents and grandparents were monumental in developing my self-esteem. I was fortunate to grow up in a world where encouragement, praise, and love were effortlessly demonstrated. I am reminded daily in perfect ways of how incredibly important my early environment was.

To Catherine, I value the special bond that we share and our mutual commitment to reaching even greater depths of honesty and truth. She reminds me of how important it is to take life (and myself), a little less seriously at times. I am so grateful that we are together in this lifetime as sisters.

Live Your Life's Purpose was originally published in 2005 under the imprint of Orpheus Press. What you have in your hands is a "gently" revised version reflecting my study and work since that time, and the thoughtful eye of a remarkable editor who uses her innate gifts and talents each time she set eyes on a new manuscript.

I am forever indebted to Gillian Rodgerson, my editor, Graham Fidler, of Publishers Group Canada, and Mike O'Connor, publisher of Insomniac Press, for seeing the potential of my original work and for collectively bringing this revised edition to the world.

To all of my clients, past and present, I am privileged to hear your most intimate and significant life experiences, and to be witness to your remarkable journeys. It is through my work with you that I continue to learn, and remain humbled by your incredible courage to heal. It has been through my work with you that I have learned how to fully live my purpose. A heartfelt "thank you" to the many clients who allowed me to share their stories in the pages that follow.

FOREWORD

From where I sit at my desk, I look out onto a beautiful freshwater lake. I watch as different species of birds fly among the trees. Several land effortlessly on the swaying branches of the nearby maples. And then moments later, they soar off again, their wings easily taking them where they want to go. The wonderful thing about these birds is that they live their purpose daily. In fact, they spend a significant amount of time flying—doing what they were created to do.

As human beings, we've made life far too complicated. We've evolved intellectually but at the expense of our instinctive abilities and our sacred connection with our inner self. It's as though we have forgotten how to enjoy each present moment of beauty and wonderment and instead spend much of the present reliving the past or contemplating the future. In those fleeting moments when our mind is quiet, we experience an unfamiliar and uncomfortable emptiness or void. And then just like that, we become consumed again with our thoughts. Thinking takes us easily out of the present moment and far away from our inner voice which intuitively has the answer. If we spend any amount of time with our self in silence, it becomes clear: beneath what we perceive as emptiness lies truth.

If we can learn how to listen, a whole new world opens to us. It is here, we discover that from quiet comes a sense of calm and inner peace that is indeed the opposite of empty. Rather, the inner quiet that we begin to experience is our spirit (our life force). Our intuitive wisdom waits to guide us as long as we dare to listen.

If you are awakening to the desire to become something *more,* then I encourage you to use this guidebook as an instrument to show you how to go within yourself for answers. Contemplate the ideas and experience the exercises as if you were following a road map—bringing you back to yourself.

Know that there *is* perfection in the purpose of your life and in the events that shape it. The moments of your life become far more personally meaningful when you identify your purpose. Reading this book, I hope that you will be inspired to think differently about yourself and your life. The consciousness that you will bring to each moment makes it possible to begin experiencing your own life differently, and to be compelled to live it in a way that honours your spirit.

INTRODUCTION

We are living in a time of great spiritual awakening. Mankind has evolved from a creature with a basic need to hunt, gather, and procreate as a means of survival, to a higher consciousness with independent and contemplative thought. We live in a sophisticated world and yet one that concurrently reminds us of our humble origins. Sudanese tribes on the western bank of the Nile, living an uncomplicated existence, share the planet with the busiest urban centers of New York and Beijing. As residents of the economically developed world, we can travel to distant places and be reacquainted with our evolutionary and spiritual roots, or live our entire lifetimes wrapped in the illusions of material goods, power, and privilege.

What we choose is fundamentally based on our individual evolution. In order to consider the possibility of living our life's purpose, we need to reach a level of consciousness that goes beyond preoccupation with the day-to-day rudimentary activities of our lives. Personal growth begins with the discipline of heightened awareness of our self and the desire to evolve—to become "more." With the insight and confidence that we gain from following a path that is influenced by spirit, we become inspired to build our lives around the purposeful things that we are skilled at and most enjoy; we experience what it means to feel authentic happiness and we look for ways to use our gifts that positively contribute to the lives of others.

I wrote *Live Your Life's Purpose* with the intention of creating a guidebook—a manual for initiating greater self-awareness for the purpose of intentional evolution. The ideas that I speak of come out of my own study, training, and experience as a psychotherapist and from what I *live*. There is a great deal to be experienced the moment you commit to self-improvement and personal integrity. You will continue to be challenged by all that you seek to master, reminding you of the magnitude of each single moment as being critical for practicing truth, honesty, and love.

With greater consciousness comes the knowledge that your inner happiness is derived from feeling good about who you are on a core level. Inner happiness comes from sharing your authentic self with others, but in order to share authentically, you must know your inner self and feel good about who that self is.

Conscious awareness is the mechanism that allows you to look closely at all aspects of your self. As you do this, you begin to identify what it is that makes you happiest. From there, you can consciously begin to navigate your life toward what brings this happiness and sense of fulfillment. This is **living authentically**. Consciousness presupposes that you will continue working on your inner self as you live authentically. In fact, it becomes far more difficult (and inwardly uncomfortable) to ignore your previous way of being once you begin to see yourself as you really are. Living consciously means that you will continue to face the often daunting task of identifying what it is that you want to change or improve. To embrace the notion that there will always be work to do as you choose to evolve your inner self means that you can be more accepting of and patient with your progress.

Creating positive change is empowering. Seeing even small progress toward what you desire, it becomes easier to share your inner self with others. As you share your inner, authentic self, you will begin to feel inwardly validated. Feeling good about being honest with yourself and others about who you are, you will surround yourself with people who embrace and accept the positive changes you're making.

As you move toward a greater level of individual consciousness, you are more likely to recognize that you have a specific purpose. If you pay close attention, you will see the connection between what you are instinctively good at, what you enjoy, and what nourishes your inner self. Recognizing your life's purpose means you can be your authentic self all the time and share who you are and what you have to offer with others.

The first section of this book is designed to encourage you to explore your current self, to identify the aspects of your inner self that require attention, and to help you create change and feel a far greater sense of happiness and fulfillment. The second section focuses on discovering your life's purpose. It identifies the elements of inner wisdom and life lessons and the notion of your *gifts*—all of which serve to clarify and shape your specific purpose in this world. The final section offers guiding principles for staying connected to your inner self and living your life's purpose each day.

Use a journal to record your responses to the exercises found throughout the book as well as to contemplate the ideas and insights that you gain.

Section One

CHAPTER ONE

Consciousness

Without consciousness, we cannot begin any journey. Consciousness precedes inner knowledge and inner knowledge precedes right, positive action.

The Art of Conscious Awareness

To be consciously aware requires you to be fully observant of yourself (your inner thoughts, feelings, and behaviors), others, and your surroundings. Conscious awareness is the direct path to self-honesty and truth. You see things *as they are* rather than convincing yourself of what you need them to be. Being conscious, you are aware of the anxiety that comes from thoughts of self-denial and avoidance. You may not like the feeling of anxiety, but your ability to be conscious allows you to observe your experience in that moment rather than ignore or repress what you feel. When you experience yourself honestly, you can choose to react with full awareness.

With conscious awareness of *what is* comes the ability to live authentically. Because you are choosing to observe situations and events in your life with honesty, you are no longer willing to justify your behaviour (or someone else's) in order to feel better. In fact, feeling remorseful for actions that don't necessarily reflect who you are or how you want to be helps you to make some honest choices for the future.

To create any kind of change, you must be aware of how you are.

Consciousness breeds positive change because it requires you to take a good look at yourself at times when you feel an uncomfortable emotion.

Drew's story is a clear example of this. Quick to anger, Drew said that he had neither patience nor tolerance for people who didn't take their job seriously. A supervisor of seasonal staff at a large amusement park, Drew explained that he would constantly find fault with his staff's behaviour. Drew's boss had suggested he seek my help because his boss was concerned that he was "micromanaging his staff in a critical and not constructive way." Drew admitted that he had deliberated for some time before calling me. He confessed that he didn't really understand why he needed to work with me.

As Drew began to talk, it was clear that he had very strong ideas about how his staff should treat park guests. When he saw a staff member behaving in a way that didn't meet his own high standard, Drew would immediately address the employee, but without awareness of the negative way in which he did so. While Drew's main focus was providing excellent customer service, his behaviour was largely perceived by staff and guests as overbearing and critical. Drew's first step before making any change was to become consciously aware of his self.

Present Moment Awareness

Your **present moment awareness** allows you to live consciously. When you are fully present, your attention is focused in that moment. For example, when you are folding laundry you are simply folding laundry. As you take your dog for a walk through the park you are simply walking. You are aware of your surroundings, using your senses to experience fully each moment, but that is all. Your focus remains in the present moment.

Being fully present makes you an observer. You observe your inner self (your thoughts, feelings, and physical sensations) as well as all that is external to you. Being present allows you to be aware without being attached to or distracted by what is occurring in that moment. You observe the sky to be grey and overcast without wishing it were different. You do not become caught up in thoughts such as how miserable the weather has been this week or that you should have remembered to bring in the outdoor furniture cushions because now they will be ruined. Present moment awareness is observing *without judgment*.

Conscious awareness means you can recognize the difference between moments when you are simply *being*, and times when you are busy analyzing a particular situation, contemplating the future, or thinking of the past.

*Being conscious does not preclude
thinking about past events or
anticipating future moments. Rather, it
allows you to recognize when you are in
the present moment and when you are
not: in the present moment, you simply
fully experience everything
in that moment.*

To practice present moment awareness, pay attention to what you're thinking, feeling, and doing in a particular moment. Recognize when you are *not* being fully aware, that is, when you are caught up in thoughts that take you out of the present. For most of us, being out of the present moment is far *more familiar* than being in it. Use your conscious awareness to help you return to the present.

Living in the present is a challenge because of our well-established attachment to what we have devised as chronological time. At least since the development of the ancient Egyptian calendar, which recorded 4236 BC as the earliest year in history, humankind has been preoccupied with measuring and recording the passage of time. For the most part, we eat, sleep, work, and play according to a specific, *time enforced* schedule. As the establishment of "standard time" is useful (and necessary) in the practical aspects of life,

*Recognize the importance of repeatedly
bringing yourself back to the present in
order to experience your life as a series of
moments.*

How much of your life is spent living in either past or future moments? How often do you go to work thinking about what you need to do that day, or what you have planned for later that evening rather than experiencing present moment awareness? As you travel to work, how much time do you spend being consciously aware of your surroundings and how you currently feel?

How often do you only partially listen as your kids talk about their day, your mind already thinking ahead to what you are going to prepare for dinner or the fact that you forgot to put the garbage out that morning? Do you go to bed at night replaying the intriguing conversation you had earlier that day with your best friend or being fully present as your head touches the soft pillow and your muscles begin to relax, feeling your body fully supported by the mattress beneath? *In fact, we rarely allow ourselves to be fully present in each moment.*

Living the majority of our lives outside of the present moment feels effortless largely because we have become so skilled at allowing our thinking brain—our analytical self—to take over. We literally live *in our heads* as opposed to being fully conscious of our self and our surroundings. We have learned how to react rather than observe. We feel compelled to be "productive" by *doing* rather than *being* still and quiet.

In truth, we actually experience little of our lifetime as it is happening.

In a world where multi-tasking and time-tracking are considered acceptable and necessary ways of being, living in the present has become the anomaly. Whether you're cracking eggs into a sauté pan or moving your body into a specific posture during a yoga class, it is when you make an effort to pay attention to what you are doing in each moment that you experience the moment fully. These become *your* moments.

While it can be helpful (and is certainly necessary) at times, to think about the past (to review, assess, understand), or the future (to plan, organize, and visualize), in the present moment you are simply experiencing. In the present, there is no worry or anxiety about the future (remember—the future hasn't happened yet!) and there is neither guilt nor regret based on past events. In the present moment, you are simply *being*. You exist. The next time that you feel an uncomfortable emotion, the impulse to react with anger or aggression, or feelings of annoyance or frustration, observe what happens when you move yourself back into the present. Rather than become caught up in "the story" that you have convinced yourself is true, notice how you feel when you pull your attention back into the present.

DAILY PRACTICE: PRESENT MOMENT AWARENESS

Several times during your day, make it a practice to move your attention out of the past or future. Step out of the time dimension of thinking, analyzing, and judging what you *perceive* to be true.

Instead, be present as a silent observer of your mind.

Know that being fully present requires effort. It takes discipline and practice to recognize when you are not in the present moment and to bring your attention into now.

Practice present moment awareness by carving out time to be quiet in order to listen within.

Being fully present allows for personal insight and discovery that is unavailable to you when you are living outside of the present moment. One of the easiest ways to listen within is by following your breath.

Conscious Breathing

I teach clients the skill of conscious breathing as a way of developing the ability to simply *observe* the present moment.

Being present is more easily accomplished through the practice of observing whatever it is that you notice as you breathe.

Observing your breath naturally brings your attention back to the present moment. Daily practice of conscious breathing helps you to develop the habit of simply *being*. It also reinforces your ability to be aware of your inner self.

Conscious breathing is a form of **meditation**. Meditation is the practice of focusing your attention on a single thing. While it sounds simple enough, most of us have never experienced what it is like to quietly observe the inner peace that comes with simply being in the present moment. Conscious breathing is one of the easiest ways to connect within and to develop your ability to experience the present.

DAILY PRACTICE: CONSCIOUS BREATHING

To begin, choose a quiet place where you can sit undistracted for a short period of time.

Creating a "sacred" place where you can feel comfortable and relaxed helps support your conscious breathing practice until it becomes well-established. Consider using this technique as part of your meditation practice.

Instead of filling spare moments with things to keep you busy, use these moments for conscious breathing. Conscious breathing allows you to return to the present moment where you experience an inner calm and a heightened sense of awareness.

Once you feel skilled at conscious breathing, you can use it any time, anywhere. You may choose to breathe consciously as you remain still, or as a compliment to other activities such as walking, driving your car in busy traffic, or waiting in line at the grocery store.

Notice what happens to your thoughts as you breathe with full consciousness. Notice how you feel after a few moments of conscious breathing.

STEP ONE: FOCUSED ATTENTION

- Place one hand on your chest over your heart, and one hand on your belly, just below the solar plexus. (Using your hands heightens your awareness).
- Bring your attention inward.
- Take a deep breath in through your nose.
- Feel your upper chest expand as air fills your lungs.
- Notice that as your chest expands, your collarbone will lift as your upper chest fills and the upper back expands. Feel the hand resting over your heart move upwards and slightly away from your body.
- As you exhale, allow yourself to breathe out through your mouth, relaxing and dropping your jaw. Allow your lips to part slightly.
- Feel (and hear) your breath leave your body out through your mouth.
- Let your upper chest drop, and your upper back move in toward your spine.
- Continue breathing for the next minute with full attention on your breath as it comes in through your nose and out through your mouth.
- Feel your chest move as you breathe deep breaths.

Step Two: Felt-Sense

- As you continue breathing in through your nose and out through your mouth, bring your attention down to your stomach.
- Imagine that you have a balloon in your stomach.
- Give your balloon a colour.
- As you breathe in through your nose, imagine that your balloon is filling with air expanding outward, pushing your stomach and your hand – outward. (As you inhale, your diaphragm lowers into your belly, and your ribs expand making room for your breath). Notice how this feels.
- As you exhale through your mouth, imagine that the air is being let out of the balloon.
- As the balloon become smaller, feel your ribs release to their starting position. Finally, relax your belly back in toward your spine.

Step Three: Visualization

- Continue breathing, in through your nose, and out through your mouth. Focus on the colour of your balloon.
- Notice that as you inhale, your balloon expands, becoming lighter in colour.
- As you exhale, see and feel the air being let out of your balloon. Notice that as the balloon becomes smaller, its colour becomes darker.
- For a few more cycles of breathing, focus your attention on the colour of the balloon. Watch the colour change as you breathe in and out.

* Practice this with your eyes closed to enhance your inward focus.

The expansion in your chest that occurs when you inhale indicates that you are filling your lungs with oxygen. This pushes the diaphragm muscle downward, causing your stomach to expand. When you exhale, your stomach and chest naturally move inward, toward your body.

If you have difficulty feeling your stomach or your chest expand, remember that, like any skill, conscious breathing will take practice and patience. With some modest effort, you can master it with a few minutes of daily practice over the course of a week. Use conscious breathing at times throughout your day when you need to feel calm and centered. A few conscious breaths will create greater awareness of everything internal to your self. It will also enable you to refocus your attention to the present moment.

Conscious breathing is one way to develop present moment awareness. Make an effort to create a five-minute practice at the start of each day by simply taking several conscious breaths with your eyes closed. Remember how you felt before your breath meditation. What happened to the pangs of anxiety or the palpable dread that you might normally have experienced as you got ready for work? Did you experience any change in the intensity of these feelings? Are these feelings replaced with a sense of inner calm? Your brief meditation becomes a powerful way of quieting your busy mind and connecting within. You can make it a part of your daily regimen—like brushing your teeth.

While there are several ways to communicate with your inner self, conscious breathing is the mechanism that allows your conscious mind to quiet so you can actually *hear* your unconscious mind (or what is commonly referred to as your **inner voice**). It is in this place of quiet that you receive unsolicited thoughts, ideas, and images from your unconscious mind. Your unconscious mind provides limitless guidance, helping you make the best possible decisions. All you need to do is listen.

Using conscious breathing, you create a dominance of **alpha-wave rhythms** in the brain. This change in brain activity allows you to be simultaneously alert and relaxed.

Physiologically, these changes occur in the body at the same time as blood pressure and heart rate decrease, accompanied by an increase of oxygen to the brain. The result is a natural state of inner peace.

What would it mean to be able to define each moment? How can your conscious breathing practice help you find a more purposeful existence?

Imagine taking a few conscious breaths before contemplating your most important priorities for the day or before making essential decisions. Would conscious breathing help you to feel calmer? More self-assured?

What if you were to integrate a conscious breathing practice at specific times throughout your day as a way of refocusing your attention and feeling centered?

Without having a tool for bringing your attention back into the present, it is possible to operate on "automatic pilot" for much of your day. For example, do you ever arrive home not *fully* remembering most of your journey? If you habitually take the same route (whether by car, transit, or bicycle) it becomes easy to "zone out" of the present moment, getting distracted by the many thoughts that come into your mind. What would you notice about the *quality* of your commute if you added a conscious breathing practice? What might you become more aware of as a result?

Breathing with consciousness is the mechanism for returning your attention to the present moment.

Because you are aware, you are better equipped to find answers simply by asking within. For example, at times when you find yourself struggling with finding a solution to a problem, it can often become more difficult to make the *best* decision, since your mind is flooded with possibilities. It is here that you might close your eyes and bring your awareness into the present. Use conscious breathing to quiet your mind and to let go of all thoughts. You may have to do this for a period of several minutes or several times in order to achieve a state of calm. Ask your unconscious mind for the "right" answer and listen to the spontaneous response that comes.

Similarly, the next time you find yourself reaching for something to snack on, ask yourself: "What is it that I *really* need at this moment?" Listen to the first response that your unconscious mind gives you. Being fully conscious allows you to recognize that you are actually tired and not hungry. You can use this awareness to take a nap rather than eat.

Ancient yogis living in the forests and mountain regions of India had intimate contact with nature. Studying the breathing rate of wild animals, they discovered that those with a slow breathing rate (snakes, crocodiles, elephants, and tortoises) have a long lifespan. Conversely, they noticed that animals with a fast breathing rate (such as birds, cats, dogs, and rabbits) lived for only a few years. Realizing the importance of slow breathing, yogis measured a person's lifespan, not in years but by the number of breaths. They considered that each individual is allocated a fixed number of breaths in their lifetime. Therefore, if a person breathes slowly and deeply, they not only gain more vitality but they also optimize their experience of life.

Whether or not you believe that the ancient yogis were right, recognize that nature can teach us much about living purposefully. Know that you feel far calmer and centered when you take deep, *conscious* breaths.

Conscious breathing is the mechanism that allows you to let go of the barrage of noise created by your thinking, analytical brain. It is *in the moment* that you can observe and experience—without judgment.

When you are in the present there are no thoughts—you are simply being.

You *live* in each moment. Conscious breathing is a fundamental practice for living a far more purposeful life.

CONSCIOUS THINKING

To think consciously is to bring awareness to your thoughts. While this seems relatively easy in theory, most of us are not skilled at *consciously experiencing* what we say to our self. Rather, it feels as though our thoughts have a life of their own.

We interpret our thoughts as being in control of what we think about, rather than viewing our mind as the creator of our thoughts.

To practice conscious thinking means making deliberate choices about what we think about. It also requires us to understand how our thoughts determine everything.

One of the basic principles of Cognitive Therapy helps to explain the connection between what we think about and how we feel and react:

Thoughts ⇨ Feelings ⇨ Behaviours

Thoughts are your ongoing internal dialogue. Your thoughts include your perceptions, assumptions, and your interpretation of a situation. Because many of us are "visual dominant," together with our thoughts we also *see* images or pictures flash across our mind.

*Your thoughts and images
create your feelings.*

Feelings can be described by a single word: "happy," "sad," "angry," "guilty," and "anxious" are only some of the many feelings we have. We often use the words "feelings," "moods," and "emotions" interchangeably to represent how we *feel*.

Your feelings create your behaviours.

Behaviours are *what you do*. They are your actions and reactions: "crying," "avoiding others," and "working late" are all examples of behaviours.

Your thoughts, feelings, and behaviours are all interconnected, and yet, everything begins with your thoughts.

Let's take a closer look at how it all works. Consider the following "thought record," that occurred in Deborah's head when she realized that she hadn't heard from her best friend in more than a week.

"I wonder why Sonya hasn't called me?"
"Maybe I said something in our last conversation that offended her."
"What if she's upset with me."
"I bet she wouldn't even tell me if I said something that offended her."

"Maybe I'm not as important to her as her other friends."

"I guess our friendship isn't as strong as I thought."

Whether any of these thoughts are actually true isn't as important as the fact that Deborah automatically accepted her thoughts *as real* possibilities. As a result, she felt:

- confused
- sad
- worried
- annoyed

Deborah's feelings affected her behaviours. She decided to:
- avoid calling Sonya (in case Sonya really was upset with her) since Deborah was uncomfortable with conflict;
- call their mutual friend Natalie to see if she knew anything;
- be reserved and detached if Sonya did call— after all, she doesn't seem to really care about their friendship.

When I helped Deborah track her thoughts, she was able to examine how her thoughts affected her feelings and subsequent behaviours. Deborah admitted feeling silly. Allowing her thoughts to *create* a story that wasn't based on any factual evidence was revealing for Deborah.

Your thoughts are incredibly powerful.

You create and experience specific emotions because of what you say to yourself. Your emotions invoke a reaction that is based on what you believe to be true.

In fact, much of the time, there is little or no *evidence* to suggest that your perception of the situation is indeed accurate.

Connecting Thoughts, Feelings, and Behaviours

As Deborah made the connection between what she said to herself (her thoughts) and her feelings, she realized that she really hadn't given Sonya a chance. She recognized the distress she had caused herself in creating a story in her mind about what she thought was the truth. Making the connection between her thoughts, feelings, and behaviours was life changing for Deborah. Realizing that she was on her way to actually *creating* a problem in her friendship with Sonya helped her to look at the situation from a different perspective. Deborah began to see that she *often* created a story in her mind based on her subjective view of a situation.

Paying attention to your thoughts in any given moment, helps you to understand why you feel (and react) the way you do.

Out of present moment awareness comes the realization that you actually control what you feel and do by how you think.

If you practiced present moment awareness, what would your thoughts reveal? What emotions typically drive your behaviour?

Use the principle of *thoughts* ➪ *feelings* ➪ *behaviours*, to remind you to pay attention to your thoughts and perceptions as a first step in changing how you feel and react in any given moment.

Deborah had a voicemail waiting for her when our session was finished. It was Sonya. Sonya explained that her mother had taken ill and been rushed to hospital by ambulance. She had jumped in her car and driven the 425 km distance, the instant she received word of her mother's condition. Sonya apologized for not calling sooner but explained that she was emotionally and physically exhausted. Her mother's condition had improved even though she had been critically ill for several days. Sonya had made arrangements to stay with her parents for another week before returning to the city.

Realize that your biased perceptions can create an unrealistic version of the truth. Pay attention when you create plausible arguments that convince you your story is true. Remember that you always react based on what you believe—even when the truth is quite different.

With conscious awareness of your thoughts, comes the ability to change them. At first, it will be easier to notice when you are feeling an uncomfortable or "negative" feeling, and then work your way back to uncovering your thoughts in that moment. You do this by simply asking, "What was I just thinking about?" This is how you **track your thoughts**. Remember, you need to be aware of your thoughts before you can do anything to change them.

DAILY PRACTICE: CONNECTING THOUGHTS, FEELINGS, AND BEHAVIOURS

Practice tracking your thoughts using the exercise that follows:

- Think of a recent situation in which you remember feeling a strong negative emotion. Describe the situation briefly below.
- Now recall several of the thoughts or images that crossed your mind in that particular moment. Record these.
- Next, remember how you felt. (You may recall only one emotion or several).
- Finally, write down what your behaviours were. What you are doing here is making the connection between your thoughts, feelings, and behaviours.

The Situation:

My Thoughts ⇨   My Feelings ⇨   My Behaviours

By paying attention to your automatic thoughts in any given situation, you can gain insight into *why* you behaved the way you did, or *why* you are feeling a certain way. Begin to practice tracking your thoughts as part of your present moment awareness.

For Drew, completing a *thought record* in different situations when he felt angry was truly revealing. Previously unaware of how his abrasive and punitive behaviour affected his staff, Drew was now able to see how his angry feelings would compel him to react abruptly. Understanding the need to be conscious of his thought process meant that Drew could begin to *challenge* his thoughts when he began to feel angry.

With consciousness comes the ability to change your thoughts.

Challenging your thoughts is the most effective way to change how you feel.

To do this, you need to be willing to deconstruct the story you have convinced yourself is true.

When you first begin to track your thoughts, it's important to record them as accurately as you can. Each thought is created in less than a millisecond. We rarely have a single thought occur in isolation. When we analyze and interpret any situation, we tend to experience several thoughts in relation to what we see. Track your thoughts with the knowledge that you may need to work at remembering *all* of the different things you said to yourself at any given time.

Below is Drew's thought record with examples of how he challenged his automatic thoughts.

The Situation:

Seeing three staff talking together in front of the concession stand. Only one person is serving customers and there is a small lineup waiting to place orders.

My Thoughts ⇨	My Feelings ⇨
"*What* do they think they're doing? Why are they just standing around talking when customers are waiting for service?"	* irritated, annoyed
"I knew I should never have put Jeremy and Alex in the concession. Those two are always goofing off when they work together."	* frustrated, angry
"I hate that I always have to deal with this stuff!"	*angry
"I wish that just for once the staff would actually take their jobs seriously!"	* infuriated, annoyed

I asked Drew to challenge each of his thoughts using the sentence stem,
"Where's the evidence?....."

Challenging your thoughts this way forces you to look for actual evidence that supports your line of thinking. Finding evidence to refute your original thought is easier than you might think.

The following shows how Drew challenged his thoughts:

My Thoughts:

"*What* do they think they're doing? Why are they just standing around talking when customers are waiting for service?"

Challenging My Thoughts:

"Where's the evidence that.... they are *just* standing around?

My Hints to Drew: • Did you happen to find out what they were discussing? (Drew responded that he had not).
• Could they be discussing something related to work?
• Is it possible that they might have been sorting out a customer problem?
• Would they really be just standing around in front of customers?

My Thoughts:

"I knew I should never have put Jeremy with Alex

in the concession. Those two are always goofing off when they work together."

Challenging My Thoughts:
"Where's the evidence that.... Jeremy and Alex always goof off when they work together?"

Note: Drew *did* remember that Jeremy and Alex actually worked quite well together when they trained a new employee the week before. He was actually quite pleased with how well they did.

My Thoughts:
"I hate that I always have to deal with this stuff!"

Challenging My Thoughts:
"Where's the evidence that.... I *always* have to deal with this stuff ?"
My Hints to Drew: I asked him if "always" was an accurate estimate. "Weren't there days when his staff worked well?"

My Thoughts:
"I wish that just for once the staff would actually take their jobs seriously!"

Challenging My Thoughts:
"Where's the evidence that.... the staff *don't* actually take their jobs seriously!"

Note: Drew was able to realize that he was thinking in "all or nothing" terms again. He admitted that there were many occasions when the staff handled situations very responsibly—and without his help!

In each case, Drew could not find any *actual* evidence to prove that his original thoughts were accurate. In fact, when we examined other possibilities (see "Notes" and "Hints") and points of view, Drew realized that his original thoughts were actually a poor estimation of what turned out to be the truth: Jeremy and Alex were attending to Erik, who had come to them looking for Drew. Erik had a deep cut in his left leg because he had fallen off the roof of one of the adjacent buildings while doing maintenance on one of the rides. He needed Drew's permission to go the hospital.

CHAPTER TWO

The Search for Self: The Inner Journey

Knowing your self comes from going within. It means being willing to (consistently) take a hard look at who you currently are—and then being willing to do the work that is necessary to improve upon that.

*The journey within is all
about self-knowledge.*

It is through self-awareness and self-responsibility that you see the various experiences of your life as challenges to grow—to become more. our search for self is a conscious journey. You choose exactly how much awareness you bring to all aspects of yourself. You choose to live with your eyes wide open, willing to see yourself exactly as you are or perhaps unwilling to be fully honest.

*Your life becomes a representation
of your honesty with yourself.*

How well you are willing to know yourself becomes the metaphor for your life. Your truth *does* set you free. Your ability to be truthful with yourself and others determines the quality of authenticity that you live by.

As you embrace the information and knowledge that comes with being fully aware, you realize that the inner journey—the *search for self*—continues throughout your lifetime. The search for self is indeed limitless.

Your search for self may occur as a result of a gnawing feeling that there is something more that you can do with your life. It may grow out of your desire to feel better about who you are. It may be a guided process that you accept with the help of a loved one, a trusted friend, or a therapist. It may come as the result of a specific life experience—perhaps positive but more often one that is personally challenging and difficult. Yet, at the root of your search for self is a desire to create a specific change.

Your search for self is innately tied both to your level of conscious awareness and your self-esteem. The higher your level of healthy self-esteem and self-awareness, the greater your desire for self-knowledge and discovery. The more you discover and learn, the greater the momentum for change and evolution. Your level of healthy self-esteem grows directly out of your enhanced knowledge of your self (through your ability to be fully conscious), and your intention and effort to improve all that you already are.

SELF-ESTEEM

Your self-esteem defines you. It influences every aspect of your life at all times.

Self-esteem characterizes how you think, see, and feel about yourself. Your level of self-esteem is correlated to your level of self-worth (the level to which you value yourself). Self-esteem is who and what you believe yourself to be. Self-esteem can be measured by the following three elements:

Self-concept
How you *think* about your self.

Self-image
How you *see* your self.

Felt-sense
How you *feel* in relation to your self.

(The emotions and physical sensations that characterize how you experience your self.)

By nurturing consistently positive experiences in each of these elements, you develop healthy *self-es-*

teem and a positive *sense of self*. Self-esteem is important to nurture and build upon throughout your lifetime.

Your belief in your abilities and the confidence you possess stems from the psychological development of your self-esteem. As a child, your self-esteem is initially developed and nurtured by parents and caregivers within your family of origin. If you were blessed with supportive, loving parents who had healthy levels of self-esteem themselves then it is likely that you entered adulthood possessing a high level of self-esteem. But even if your early development of self-esteem was compromised, you are always able to increase your level of healthy self-esteem. You nurture and grow your self-esteem as a direct result of the *inner work* that you do.

Positive self-esteem presupposes consciousness. When you make the conscious effort to build your self-esteem, you inherently increase your capacity for self-awareness and introspection. Positive self-esteem inspires you to become more.

You put attention and effort into discovering and developing your abilities, talents, and innate gifts. With healthy self-esteem, you recognize that each life experience is an opportunity to learn. With awareness of what is right and best for you, you begin to move in the direction of your life's purpose.

When self-esteem is low, it can hold you back from believing that you are capable of a greater purpose. It holds you back from doing what you most want to do with your life. That was the case for Pete.

I met Pete while doing a corporate presentation for the staff at his workplace. A few months later, Pete called to set up an appointment with me. One of the first things I remembered about him was how easily he had made others around him laugh.

The Pete who arrived at my office was a completely different person. His face was sunken; he had dark circles around his eyes and he looked like he had aged about twenty years.

Pete was only twenty-six and he hated his life.

After barely scraping by in high school, Pete had spent three years working at various jobs in construction and tourism. He was now enrolled in a two-year college program in computer networking. While he recognized the benefit of obtaining a college diploma, Pete admitted that he really didn't want to spend the rest of his life working at a typical nine-to-five job. His sole reason for enrolling in school was to relieve some of the pressure he felt from his parents. His three older siblings were university students, on their way to successful careers in law, business, and education.

But Pete was miserable at the thought of living the kind of life that his parents wanted for him.

When I asked Pete what he would most enjoy doing, he replied instantly: "I want to be a landlord. I would love to own a few rental properties and look after them. I could live a comfortable life doing that and I would be my own boss."

Pete knew what he wanted to do with his life. His parents were wealthy, and it was quite possible that they would be willing to provide him with a loan in order to help him buy his first property.

Pete's biggest roadblock wasn't finding a way to fund his dream; rather, he needed to believe in himself. He needed to be committed and focused enough to see his dream through to reality. He needed to stop finding excuses for why he couldn't make his dream happen and start living it.

Pete needed to build his self-esteem.

With low self-esteem, you don't fully trust your own abilities.

Intellectually, you might recognize that you *should be* deserving and worthy (of love, loyal friendships, financial success, and so on). Yet, on an emotional level you *don't really believe* it to be true. Your low self-esteem compels you to continually search outside of yourself for things you believe will make you happy, in part because you don't feel confident that you can provide these things for yourself. Your low self-worth means that you continue to lose yourself in all of the things you do, buy, own, desire, and want. Your low self-worth makes it difficult for you to recognize the importance of fulfilling your needs—especially when others make demands on you. Consequently, you continue to willingly put others' wants and needs before your own. When your self-esteem is low, you rely heavily on others for advice, direction, support, and knowledge. You do this because you don't trust your intuitive knowledge of what is right and best for you.

When you build self-esteem, you nurture your belief

in your self. You begin to feel confidence in yourself and in your ability to do what is best and right for you. Healthy self-esteem is necessary to move toward what makes you happiest. With positive self-esteem comes the increased ability to define and actually *live* your life's purpose.

Building Self-Worth and Self-Esteem

Fundamentally, early childhood is the critical time for building a healthy experience of self. In the early stages of development, your self-esteem grows as a function of experiencing unconditional love, positive feedback, encouragement, and support. With positive nurturing, your self-esteem has a good foundation and will flourish. By the time you reach adulthood, you have a well-established, high level of self-esteem. You are able to move through life seeking out new experiences and challenges with confidence and self-worth.

Individuals who did not have a nurturing environment for building self-esteem, or whose self-esteem has been damaged or wounded in early development, struggle to claim what has always rightfully belonged to them—their belief in their self. It is as though their potential for living life has been limited. It requires effort and work to heal psychological and emotional wounds of their past, and to overcome the challenges of building their self-esteem to a level that allows them to function more effectively in everyday life.

I was introduced to Annabel when she came to see me with her former husband, Tim. Separated for almost a year, Annabel explained that she finally gave in to Tim's urging for counselling since he was unwilling to accept the fact that she did not want to reconcile.

When she married Tim, Annabel noted, she willingly gave up all of her self.

With low self-worth (due to both the implicit as well as the spoken messages she received throughout childhood), Annabel placed less value on herself and her needs than on others'. She gave up what was important to her, replacing it with what was important to others. Over time, this self-effacing behavior had left Annabel with little of herself.

By leaving Tim, Annabel could reclaim her self. She recognized that her inconsolable depression, her growing resentment toward Tim, and the large inner void she felt would eventually destroy her. She saw reclaiming her self as saving herself.

Perhaps the greatest gift a parent can give their child is instilling high self-worth and self-esteem.

Even without understanding the concept of self-esteem, children inherently *know* if a parent has good self-esteem, or conversely, if they do not. With a healthy level of self-esteem, your words and actions are congruent. Since children learn far more from what they see you do than from what you say, they learn important *self-worth behaviours* simply by observing. Healthy levels of self-esteem and self-worth become far easier to instill in your child if you yourself have them.

Annabel spent the next six months working with me in individual therapy. She chose to file for divorce only after she had been able to emotionally disengage her feelings of responsibility and guilt. For so long, Annabel had wanted to leave her marriage but claimed she felt responsible for Tim. Learning how to "unplug" from an overwhelming sense of responsibility was cathartic for Annabel. She learned to give of herself to her friends and family *while still* (rather than *instead of*) honouring her needs.

Visualize a horizontal line in your mind's eye. Make this your internal measure of self-esteem. Even though the line you see has definite starting and ending points, know that self-esteem and self-worth have infinite capacity for growth. If your rating of self-esteem is higher as you travel further to the right, consider where on your imaginary line your current level of self-esteem would be. Now, think of your horizontal line as moving an infinite distance toward the right.

———————————————————▶

Your self-esteem has an infinite capacity for growth. Consider that self-esteem is a valuable concept to work on for the rest of your life.

No matter where you begin, there are no limits to growing healthy self-esteem. Consider the five strategies that follow as essential building blocks for nurturing and building self-esteem:

1) Acknowledge all of your positive qualities.

Make an effort to think about all that you value, admire, respect, and appreciate about your self. To build self-esteem, consider adding to your list over time and as you continue to think of and develop additional positive qualities. Your final list will integrate responses from both yourself *and* others.

DAILY PRACTICE: MY POSITIVE ATTRIBUTES

Write down the things about yourself that make you the most proud. (Feel free to brag a little because the list is for your eyes only.)

Remember that building self-esteem begins with reminding yourself about all of the qualities that already say you're a *good person*—particularly those qualities that contribute to acts of generosity and kindness.

With your list complete, now choose others you trust to give you honest and fair answers. Ask them to identify your positive traits and qualities. Record their responses on a separate list and compare.

How did it feel to have others comment on what they viewed as your positive qualities?

2) Acknowledge all of your personal accomplishments.

DAILY PRACTICE: MY PERSONAL SUCCESSES

Create a historical list of all of your accomplishments and successes from your earliest memory. (Again, feel free to brag a little because the list is for your eyes only.)

With your list complete, choose at least one person from your family of origin who will give you honest and fair answers. Ask them to identify your personal accomplishments and successes. If you have chosen a parent or an older sibling, it is likely that they may recall successes from your childhood that you do not remember. Ask the same question of a close friend or your partner. Record their responses on a separate list and compare.

Imagine some of your future accomplishments. Create another list recording what you hope to accomplish within the next five years, ten years, and beyond.

Your personal successes are your own. They include the accomplishments, innate talents (or gifts), and behaviours you feel most proud of.

One of the most powerful ways to build self-esteem is through acknowledging your personal successes. By reflecting on what you feel proud of, you reinforce positive feelings about your self.

3) Challenge yourself to grow by creating new experiences, learning, and achieving new goals.

You compel yourself to increase your level of healthy self-esteem by creating new experiences that force you to go beyond what you would normally do. Knowledge and learning, whether through formal channels or self-directed study, provide you with new information and feelings of pride and self-worth.

You continue to build self-worth and self-esteem throughout your lifetime by continually achieving new goals. Consider specific goals that reflect different areas of your life and with varying timelines for achievement. Setting goals in this way provides a focus and direction for creating the life you wish to live—and for developing a blueprint for how you want to begin experiencing your self. Having specific goals in place requires you to think consciously about what you want to achieve. It also forces you to think about the kind of person you want to become. Your conscious intentions help you to stay focused on your goals, as well as to periodically reassess their importance.

Daily Practice: Achieving My Goals

Consider the following questions based on a goal of personal development. Record your answers for each of the following questions using these varying timeframes:

in... **Six months**
One year
Five years

1.) How do I want to *think* about myself? *See* myself? *Feel* about myself?
2.) What do I need to do to create this?
3.) How will I monitor my progress?
4) What will an enhanced sense of self allow me to experience?

Record your responses to the following questions in as much detail as possible.

* Consider other areas of your life e.g. health, your love relationship, family, personal wealth, friends, travel, and so on. What questions could you ask that would help you achieve more in each of these areas?

4) Be honest with yourself and others.

Building healthy self-esteem has everything to do with being honest and truthful with yourself.

Honesty requires acknowledgement of what is. The more comfortable you feel practicing self-honesty, the easier it is to be honest with others.

Practice **speaking your truth**, even when it means that others will likely disagree with you. Sharing your opinion when you know others will have a different perspective says that you value what you believe—just as you value it when others are honest with you.

Daily Practice: Self-Honesty

Practice *being* the kind, loving, caring, considerate, and thoughtful person you are at your core. In sharing your authentic self with others, see the positive effect of your kind words, your smile and your ability to be honest and *real*. As you feel more confident about revealing your true self to others, pay attention to how your honesty supports the potential for more authentic relationships.

5) Strive to become your ideal self.

It is when you are willing to look at yourself with your eyes wide open that you are able to make changes. Self-esteem grows as a function of our willingness to improve upon who we are. Working on aspects of your self that you are less happy about says that you believe in yourself. You willingness to become more helps to raise your self-esteem.

Daily Practice: My Ideal Self

Create a list of the most important qualities that you want to possess.

For example:
    (1) to become confident and secure in making all of my own decisions so that I will rely less on family and friends for advice;

    (2) to have greater patience and tolerance with my loved ones;

    (3) to be more open minded to others' differences. (You can continue to add to your list as you choose.)

For each of these qualities, write down at least two action steps that will bring you closer to having these qualities as your own.

For example:
    (1)   i. Catch myself when I feel the urge to call a friend to ask for help making a decision and instead decide on my own.
        ii. After making a decision, trust that it will

be the right one without deliberating for hours.

(2)   i. Recognize when I am in a bad mood or tired after a long day's work and when I may be more vulnerable to being moody or short with those who are closest to me.
ii. Recognize if I become impatient or irritated and take a few calming breaths. Choose to make only positive instead of negative comments.

(3)   i. Ask questions to understand others' differences better.
ii. Find something in common with another person even when I think they are very different than me.

As you encounter various situations, your action step planning will help you to keep in mind how you choose to be. Notice how your conscious awareness plays an important role in enabling you to carry out these action steps.

Your inner journey begins as you embrace and explore who you really are. Your journey continues as long as you have the conscious intention to develop and evolve.

SELF-EVOLUTION

Self-evolution is about the highest level of personal growth and development. Your evolution comes out of your conscious awareness of the qualities and aspects of your self that you are unhappy with.

Self-evolution requires that you actively seek out the personal changes that reflect your ideal self.

At times, working to create permanent changes can be daunting. Individuals may choose therapy as a means of exploring the changes they have been struggling to make. Seeking a qualified professional for validation, support, and help with making a desired change can make the difference between struggling alone for a long time and achieving the desired result. While there may be a catalyst—a particular life event or circumstance that propels people into seeking such help—typically they have been thinking about making a positive life change for some time. While positive life changes can come out of prolonged feelings of anxiety, depression, anger or hopelessness, you must ultimately feel that you *deserve* much more. Intuitively, you search for inner happiness and contentment when you begin to believe that you *deserve* to experience these positive states more of the time.

The roadblocks to self-evolution are low self-esteem and the inherent fear of what change will signify. With low self-esteem, a loveless, demoralizing relationship takes a great deal of courage to step away from. Even as you know that you need to leave, it is often more scary not knowing what lies ahead.

Choosing to evolve affects the lives of your loved ones. You can't help but create even a mild whirlwind as you make changes to the way you think, speak and interact with others. For example, standing up for yourself when your angry spouse is belligerent or demoralizing affects your partner's behaviour. You may be in for a bigger battle if your move to empowerment sparks additional conflict or you may be pleasantly relieved to see that standing up for yourself means that the intimidating behaviour ceases.

> *All of us have the capacity to evolve as human beings.*

We evolve our consciousness by bringing attention to our thoughts and feelings—and by developing a greater awareness of the consequences of our actions. We evolve our sense of self as we seek to know who we are and trust in our *self* and our abilities. We experience authentic happiness as we seek to define and live in our truth.

Individuals who are highly evolved work from **a place of spirit** much of the time. They are consciously and intuitively aware of the impact of their words and behaviours on others. They are able to recognize when their actions are influenced by ego and quickly work to behave instead as their authentic self. Highly evolved individuals are able to give of their self, operating from a place of compassion on a daily basis. They see beyond the *humanness* of this planet and look for opportunities to connect with others in a special and meaningful way. By living their life's purpose, highly evolved people feel a deep sense of gratitude as they fulfill their destiny.

Section Two

CHAPTER THREE

Finding Meaning and Purpose

Out of doing what you feel most passionate about,
you create meaning and purpose for your life.

With consciousness comes the desire to seek more—for yourself and your life. You believe that there is more for you to experience and enjoy then what you currently have in your life. Meaning and purpose are intrinsically felt qualities, akin to feeding your soul.

Feeling purposeful is fundamentally experienced when we observe our actions affecting another living being in a positive way.

Do you *yearn* for something more for your life? What contributes to your experience of feeling purposeful? What aspects of your life currently provide you with a sense of fulfillment? What allows you to feel a sense of worth and value?

Fundamentally, you affect others by your choice to be any or all of the qualities you believe are honourable. You inspire others when you lead by example. It isn't about invoking change but rather *being the change you want to see.* By choosing to define your own purpose in this world you instill hope in others. When you create a life that is meaningful, happiness is effortless.

The Art of Happiness

Happiness is the natural state of our spirit. A central theme of Buddhist and Hindu teaching, happiness is a reflection of *dharma*—living in accordance with our life's purpose. When our choices and behaviours reflect our truth, we easily experience authentic happiness. With the potential to experience a natural state of happiness, how is it that happiness seems to elude us?

Possibly the bigger truth is simply the fact that we work hard at making ourselves unhappy. We look for complex solutions to simple problems and we create complex problems by overlooking simple solutions. Entirely unaware of our constant stream of irrational and critical ***self-talk***, we impose unrealistic expectations on ourselves, based on inaccurate and unhealthy comparisons of our self to others. We expend a vast amount of emotional and physical energy experiencing a plethora of unpleasant emotions (e.g. anxiety, fear, anger, guilt, shame) as the result of unconscious adherence to established rules and beliefs. We react by searching outside of our self for the illusionary "something" that we believe will *make us* happy.

When you look to material goods, physical pleasures, and other people to "make" you feel good, these external sources of pleasure and comfort only *momentarily* sustain you. You need to continue acquiring *more* material goods, *more* physical pleasures, and *more* external rewards to recreate these pleasant feelings. Without healthy self-esteem and a sense of purpose, you continue to search outside of your self for what you believe will make you happy. Realize instead that what you need is to go within, to connect with your inner self, and to give of your spirit.

Essentially, we could learn a thing or two from the Tibetan monks who have consciously chosen to live a highly simplified and conscious existence.

Creating authentic happiness begins by focusing within.

Carefully examine your life as it presently is. What are you aware of? What do you feel gratitude for? What is the source of your happiness now? Does your awareness force you to re-examine how you're living your life?

Daily Practice:
Observing My Current State of Happiness

Answer the following questions from a place of intuitive wisdom rather than using your analytic (thinking) brain. Do this by acknowledging the initial answer that you *feel*, rather than the answer you *think* is right.

1. "Am I happy?" (Explain)

2. "Am I happy with the person *I am*?" (Explain)

3. "What activities and experiences contribute to my authentic happiness?" (List everything that comes to mind.)

4. What aspects of *who I am* would need to change in order for me to be innately happy?

5. What aspects of my life would need to change in order for me to be innately happy?

6. "What would my life be like right now if I were able to make these changes?"

I saw Julia three months after her husband of thirty years died suddenly of a heart attack. Initially seeking help to deal with her grief, Julia soon began discussing some of the other underlying stresses that contributed to her unremitting state of unhappiness. In examining the last several years of her marriage with Ben, a chronic alcoholic, Julia realized that she had imposed several limitations on herself, making it difficult for her to feel happy. She spoke about how Ben would begin drinking when he woke up (around 2 p.m.) each day. Most nights, she confessed, he would fall asleep on the couch almost immediately after dinner. Julia restricted her own interests and hobbies to fit into her husband's schedule and admitted that even small outings, like going to a nearby coffee shop, were arduous as Ben preferred to be at home.

Julia was fuming as she relayed how Ben's ex-wife Sandra had recently served her with papers contesting Ben's will. Julia despised Sandra. A legal battle over Ben's estate was the last thing she needed. Julia, an intelligent, vivacious, and optimistic woman, was overcome with anger that first visit. Consumed by her hatred of Sandra *and* the repressed anger she now felt toward

Ben, Julia was unable to move forward in her life.

As she began to take a conscious look at how she had been living her life, Julia realized that she had been unhappy for a long time. Reminiscing about the early years of her marriage allowed Julia to remember the loving, respectful, supportive relationship that they had once shared. As our work together continued, Julia began to realize all that she had *given up* by building her life around Ben's alcoholism. Julia also acknowledged that she had rarely ever spoke up to Ben or anyone else to ask for what she needed to feel happy.

Julia needed to identify her own needs, and how to meet them for herself. She also had to use her free will to make conscious choices reflecting what was best for her. Living her life in a way that would allow her to feel *happy* again would come from being true to her inner self.

Identifying your needs (perhaps for the very first time) may be both challenging and a little scary. Even when you can identify what you need, you may continue to doubt whether you deserve to have it. At this stage, reserve any judgments. Your goal is to begin looking within, simply to identify what your needs are. This is an important part of what helps to build self-esteem and self-worth. Identifying your needs is a meaningful step towards honouring those needs. Honouring your needs is another path to happiness and self-worth.

In addition to allowing herself to grieve over Ben's death, I suggested that Julia look at her reactions toward Sandra. If she could not feel compassion toward Sandra, Julia's contempt for Ben's first wife would eventually destroy her. While she agreed with me on principle, Julia admitted that she didn't know how she would ever be able to change her feelings.

For Julia, who was so busy reacting to events outside of herself, I introduced the conscious breathing technique as a way of providing her with a means for connecting within. Each morning she would sit for ten minutes (while looking out her bay window) and breathe. Julia challenged herself to stay focused on her breath to avoid distraction. She reminded herself that her conscious mind would decide what she would think about.

As you make the conscious effort to reconnect within, you begin to create moments that are yours. Use conscious breathing as a way of focusing your attention inward, and simply *listen*. Follow your breath as a way of experiencing inner quiet. In the beginning, creating moments of quiet is enough to honour your self.

The week after she began her meditation practice, it was like a new person was sitting in my office. Julia looked visibly different—younger, with a more relaxed appearance. She no longer frowned through most of the session. Instead, her playful sense of humour had resurfaced. Julia explained that the conscious breathing was "a lifesaver." She could feel a noticeable difference in her mood state during and after her breathing practice. Julia laughed as she described her positive experiences. Through following her breath she felt calm and peaceful. Julia could feel a deep sense of inner happiness— one that she had not felt in a long time.

When you can experience the calm within you, you find the happiness that exists there also.

Feeling this innate happiness motivates you because you naturally want to extend these moments, and create many more of them. You also begin to realize that it's easier than you thought to create a life based on authentic happiness.

With a means of creating inner calm, Julia felt reconnected to her self. Experiencing authentic happiness was empowering. She practiced being conscious of her thoughts and no longer allowed her emotions to control her. Rather, Julia used the principle of *thoughts* ➪ *feelings* ➪ *behaviours* as a way of viewing Sandra's actions through Sandra's own eyes. Doing so meant that Julia no longer needed to take Sandra's behaviour personally. As we worked together over the next few months, Julia could feel herself developing compassion toward Sandra.

Authentic happiness comes from within. It develops out of the inner contentment and calm that you feel when you connect with your inner self.

Think of your inner self as your spirit— your life force.

Authentic happiness doesn't leave you simply because you had a fight with a loved one, your best friend moved across the country, or your car repair bill is several thousand dollars. Each of these circumstances may carry with it a number of other thoughts and feelings, but these events don't diminish the inner happiness you experience at your core. When you breathe, focus inwardly, and quiet your busy mind, you once again connect with the inner calm that has always been there.

Searching for happiness outside yourself becomes a never-ending quest: material goods, an expensive car, a new haircut or wardrobe, even a new relationship, give fleeting happiness. If you pay close attention, the feelings of excitement, power, confidence, and satisfaction that these things can bring are all momentary. In no time, the search for *happiness* begins yet again since the initial exhilaration you felt driving your new car has mysteriously vanished, your new haircut has grown out, and you have noticed some qualities about your new partner that you do not like.

When you've learned how to access your inner happiness, material possessions, love relationships, and vacations are all still part of your life—the difference is that you no longer rely on them for your happiness and self-worth.

I first met Lee when he was admitted into the addiction treatment centre where I worked. He told me that his drinking went out of control after his father's sudden death in an industrial accident two years earlier. Lee also had many problems in his relationship with his wife and said she abused him. He felt that she was the last person that he could rely on for support or empathy—even though he needed someone now more than ever. Lee used alcohol to cope with all of his life stress, particularly the emotional pain he was suffering as a result of his father's death.

Lee revealed that he had always lived his life doing for others *what he thought* would make *them* happy. To support his wife's demands for material possessions, in addition to his full-time job Lee worked long hours to expand a part-time business. He had been plagued with chronic anxiety and severe panic attacks for most of his adult life. Lee's self-imposed burden "to do the right thing" for everyone else—his boss, his family, his friends, and his co-workers, meant that he rarely did what *he wanted.* Even while he was able to provide his family with many luxuries, including a large home, a nice cottage, and plenty of disposable income, Lee continued to feel a deep emptiness inside. As I explained the importance of doing things that would make his self happy, I could see him struggling to comprehend my words. "I have no idea what would make me happy," he said. "I've never asked myself that question."

For Lee, acknowledging that he had never learned how to look within for happiness was an important first step.

While it is your destiny to be happy, you are responsible for creating your own happiness.

*The simplest way of creating **happiness is to live in your truth.***

This means being honest about what brings you joy. You can find meaning and purpose for your life when you can reach the happiness that exists within. Then, you can begin to consider what you need to do to create a life that relates directly to that.

Lee didn't feel worthy of putting any of his needs first. He drank to excess as a way of pushing down the anxiety and resentment that came with all of the self-imposed responsibilities. Lee began to practice conscious breathing, both as a technique to alleviate anxiety, and as a way of connecting to his inner self. Over a period of several weeks, as Lee began having small successes with his breath practice, the heart palpitations he experienced as a consequence of his acute anxiety began to dissipate. In those initial brief moments of *quiet,* Lee began to ask himself some important questions using the exercise above. I also showed Lee how to use his intuitive wisdom to make decisions based on fulfilling the needs he identified.

Your Inner Wisdom

As humans, our intellectual development has hindered our ability to listen to our inner voice. We have lost our ability to connect with our intuitiveness, relying instead on our rational or *thinking* brain for answers.

We make decisions based on what we think we *should* do, influenced largely by what society deems important. The unrealistic expectations we unconsciously live by make it extremely difficult to feel as though we are successful. By the time we reach early adolescence, the connection to our intuitive self is long lost. The honesty that was natural and effortless in childhood is replaced with a desire to prove our worth based on our perception of what society values as important.

We innocently ignore our inner wisdom and become consumed with the endless dialogue in our minds. The path within is lost.

To create a life that has meaning and purpose requires the highest level of self-honesty.

It requires that you rely on your self for answers and guidance for what's best for you.

Pay attention to the *life force* of your **innate wisdom**. Realize that the answers you search for come from within. Trusting this wisdom requires you to follow your intuitive feelings, doing what you believe is best. As the confidence to trust your inner wisdom grows, so does your self-esteem. Your ability to rely on your self means that you no longer require others to *tell* you what is best.

Be observant when you search outside of your self for answers. Use your present moment awareness to focus your attention within. Notice that any feelings of uncertainty, anxiety, or fear are replaced with a sense of calm as you hear your answer. Use your intuitive wisdom for all questions, no matter how insignificant they seem. In doing so, you strengthen the path within.

Recognize the difference between *relying* on others for answers about what is best for you and occasions when external feedback and guidance are *helpful*. For example, a loved one can be an honest observer, helping to validate what you already know or offering new insight, or a trained therapist can provide clarity and a means of thinking differently about yourself, others, and the world.

Daily Practice: Listening Within

Learn to bring your attention back into the moment in order to receive intuitive guidance about what is best and right for you. You have free will to choose what you will do in any moment, however listening within offers information from your higher self.

Begin by taking a few conscious breaths and ask: "What do I need in this moment?"

Listen for the intuitive response rather than to your thinking brain. This is what your self needs at this moment.

Honour what your self needs. Pay attention to the outcome. Honouring what your self needs at any moment goes a long way toward creating both healthy self-esteem and authentic happiness.

You can reach your inner wisdom from a place of quiet, simply using your present moment awareness to connect within. As you listen within, you may be guided to rest, spend quiet time alone, or attend to an unfinished task. As a regular daily practice, ask yourself, "What do I need today?" Your intuitive self will direct you to where you need to place your attention. You may be guided to focus on creating moments of joy, practicing kindness with others, asking for or receiving help, creating time for play, or feeling calm. Practice listening within several times throughout your day.

How helpful would it be to begin each day with a focused intention that came from your intuitive wisdom?

DAILY PRACTICE: YOUR BODY'S INTUITIVENESS

Imagine yourself doing something that you absolutely loathe. What are the physical sensations you feel in your body at this very moment? Allow yourself to experience these sensations, anchoring the feeling in your body.

Now, visualize yourself participating in an activity that you love. Notice how your body feels at this moment. Again, do your best to identify the specific physical sensations and simply experience them for a few moments. Are they different from the sensations you noted earlier? Make mental notes as you distinguish between the two felt-sense experiences. Anchoring the different inner sensations help you to *read* your body's intuitiveness at other times.

The above exercise is an ideal way to distinguish the spontaneous physiological sensations elicited simply by *what you know* to be pleasurable versus what is unpleasant. Use the felt-sense information of these experiences as a template for assessing future choices and decisions. Go *within* to read the language of your body. Your immediate physiological reaction will give you valuable information, about when you need to participate in a particular task and when you should refrain from doing so.

Let your body's intuitiveness be a source of guidance in making "right" choices and decisions for your life.

These felt-sensations are the subtle messages of your higher, intuitive self.

IDENTIFYING YOUR GIFTS

Defining what you are destined to do with your life gives you a profound sense of purpose and meaning. Your life's purpose is, to a large degree, shaped by the innate abilities and talents that are *your gifts*. Each of us has specific gifts. Your gifts are uncomplicated, often requiring little effort at best. They are not determined by intelligence, wealth, privilege, or physical attractiveness. While your gifts are predestined, you use your *free will* to decide how you share your gifts with others.

When you identify your gifts, they take on greater meaning in your life. Using your gifts, you can begin to define your life's purpose.

Daily Practice: Identifying Your Gifts

Below are useful guidelines, together with examples for how you can begin to identify *your* own special gifts:

1. **Create a list of all of the skills and abilities that come easily to you**. (e.g. writing children's stories, fixing computers, being a good listener, being well-organized). Sometimes you don't view your ability as special because you may not realize others don't have it. It's important that you include talents and skills you find easy without comparing yourself to others.

For example: You may remember that in grade school, you seemed to have the unspoken role of mediator. Other kids would come to you for help to solve conflicts. You were able to listen to both "camps" and at times to negotiate positive solutions.

Later as an adolescent, it seemed natural that your friends would come to you when they had problems. They would even remark that you always seemed to "know the right thing to do," and how they felt like you "really understood" them.

As you review situations where you have been able to help others, you will begin to uncover your gifts. In this case, your ability to listen, allowing others to *feel heard* is one of your inherent gifts. Another gift is your ability to help others find solutions to their problems.

2. **What are you inherently good at?** What abilities have always been *easy* for you? What skills and talents are you naturally gifted at? List all of these regardless of how insignificant they may seem.

For example:

Nora is a junior partner in a downtown law firm in a diverse metropolitan city. She's intelligent, ethical, and consistently empathetic with her clients. One of the professional goals that Nora identified when she began therapy was to become a senior partner in her firm. While her performance was consistently superior, Nora admitted that she still lacked some of the confidence that was needed to get to the "next level."

As we began to identify the various steps she needed to take to achieve her goal, Nora (quite by accident) identified one trait that made her stand apart from her colleagues. Nora had an inherent talent for strategic problem solving.

As Nora and I began to explore the occasions when she had used this gift, it became clear that she had completely downplayed her ability by convincing herself that others in the law firm could also do the same.

After we deconstructed several of the situations in which Nora had found herself offering strategic solutions, she began to recall positive feedback she had received from both the firm's partners and her colleagues. While she had tended to disregard their praise, Nora began to think that perhaps others *did not have* this problem-solving ability. For the first time in her life, Nora began to think about this ability as something that was special to her. Remembering her colleagues' positive comments and having senior partners acknowledge her valuable contribution helped Nora realize that this was indeed something that *she in particular* could easily offer the group. As Nora used her gift with confidence, she became more visible among the managing partners, and others increasingly looked to her for help. Sharing her gift essentially helped Nora highlight her value to the firm and take another step toward her goal of making senior partner.

3. **What do others appreciate most about you?** (Often others appreciate aspects of our self that we might not see as valuable). Recall the praise and compliments that you are consistently given. Record this. What are some of the consistent themes that could highlight a hidden gift?

   For example:
   Perhaps you have always found it easy to make others laugh. Your ability to create spontaneous humour out of situations helps to remind those around you to take themselves and life a little less seriously. Because

of this inherent ability, others seem to gravitate toward you. They enjoy your company and frequently tell you that they feel better just being around you. Your gift is your incredible sense of humour.

Look for common themes as you examine the three lists that you have created. Know that each of us is blessed with more than one gift. Remember that each of your gifts (no matter how small) serves an important purpose in your life. As you identify your particular gifts, think about how you have used them up to now. How are they helpful?

Notice what feelings you experience as you consciously use your gifts.

Recognizing your unique abilities as gifts is the first step toward living your life's purpose.

CHAPTER FOUR

Your Life's Purpose

Living your life's purpose fulfills your destiny.

Each one of us has a specific purpose for being here at this particular time. Your life's purpose (your *dharma*) is predestined. It is what you are meant to do with your life. You use your *free will* to decide how (or if) you will live your purpose.

Your life's purpose may be to identify and study a particular gene, which leads to preventing the onset of a childhood disease. It may be to write and perform music that deeply moves people. Your life's purpose may be to inspire others to think differently about themselves. It may be to save lives, to educate children, or to establish an organization that builds homes and schools for people in developing countries.

When you identify your life's purpose, you begin to make different **life choices.** You recognize that authentic happiness comes from connecting with others in a positive way as you share your self and your innate gifts. You begin to see the relevance of specific events in shaping who you are and also who you need to become. Living your life's purpose takes on a far greater meaning. You have a greater awareness of how your life's purpose affects the lives of others, and you take greater responsibility for your actions.

Discovering Your Life's Purpose

Ellen initially contacted me for career coaching. A mother of three teenage sons and step-mom to two adult sons, she was also the national executive director of a non-profit organization *and* a partner in her husband's accounting firm. Ellen admitted that she was tired of juggling such a demanding work schedule. When I asked what kind of work she might like to pursue if she could make some career changes, she became very emotional. Since Ellen had always made logical decisions based on what she thought would be the "right" thing, it was quite foreign to her to begin to think about what she might actually *like* to do with her life.

If you base your life choices predominantly on logic and practicality, those choices won't reflect what is innately best for you. Without realizing it, you will end up on a path that's not even close to what you really want to do. This was Ellen's predicament. When you ignore your intuitiveness, you almost always make the wrong choice in terms of what would make you happy.

Bring consciousness to your decision-making. *Choose* to listen inwardly to your intuitive wisdom rather than using only your intellectual mind. Trust that when you do so, you move in a direction that supports your inner happiness.

Ellen embraced these principles as she began to think consciously about the future of her career and what would make her happiest. She resigned from her position as national executive director, and stopped working for her husband's firm. Ellen began speaking about her love of drama and performing in the theatre. Taking a few months off for the first time since beginning college, Ellen spent some time catching up with her family and thinking about what she actually wanted to do with the rest of her life. She got involved in her local community theatre group and loved it so much that she started her own theatre company. A far cry perhaps from her "other world," but one that Ellen claims "completes" her. After all, "to feel as though my life has meaning and purpose was all I ever really wanted," she told me.

Defining your life's purpose and choosing to live it daily creates a meaningful and fulfilling existence. Below are ten questions that will help you to start creating what will become your life's **purpose statement**.

DAILY PRACTICE: MY LIFE'S PURPOSE STATEMENT

For each of the following sentence stems, write a minimum of six endings. The answers that come to you most immediately are from your intuitive self.

Repeat this exercise each day for one week before reading your responses.

1. I am happiest when I am...

2. If I didn't have to work for a living (and I had more money than I could ever spend), I would...

3. I feel most passionate about...

4. I feel the greatest sense of joy and fulfillment...

5. Others come to me for help with...

6. My innate gifts are ...

7. My earlier life experiences have prepared me...

8. What I most love is...

9. I have the ability to...

*10.What I have recently gone through has made me realize...

* Answer this only if you have recently experienced a major, life changing event (positive or traumatic).

Compile your answers. Look for similar key words and phrases. What are some common themes that reveal themselves? Without attempting to define a specific occupation, consider your innate contribution to the world.

Now create your life's purpose statement using the sentence stem, "My life's purpose is...."

How can you begin to live your life's purpose now? Is there a way of creating an occupation that fulfills your life's purpose statement? If so, what would you need to do? Create a list of action steps that would allow you to live your life's purpose in your working life.

Is your life's purpose different from your occupation? Do you want to bring the two closer together? How can you do this? Can you live your purpose in other ways?

If defining your life's purpose statement feels like an overwhelming task right now, it may be that you are looking too far beyond the scope of what you personally can be expected to achieve. Your life's purpose is not about creating a vaccine for cancer, ending apartheid, or attaining world peace. You might achieve any of these *as a result* of living your purpose, but your purpose itself is not about a particular end result. Rather it provides you with guidance for how you *live your life*.

Universal Purpose

The concept of a universal purpose is not entirely new. As a theoretical concept, it is found throughout the world's religions as a means of establishing the *unity* of humanity's collective moral behaviour. Unfortunately, a universal purpose that guides our moral consciousness has neither been formally established nor adopted.

Perhaps until now.

Purpose directs our choices and decisions. A *universal* purpose that transcends cultural and religious doctrines would provide a global unified directive to humanity's decision-making and altruistic behaviour. Such an objective would affirm the well-being and continuance of the human species.

Imagine a global consciousness that would provide each of us with a degree of personal meaning above and beyond what we might already possess. Considering a universal purpose could serve to evolve human consciousness for generations to come, contemplate the following three interrelated components. In striving to live by these principles, how would we change the world?

The first universal purpose is self-evolution.

Consciousness allows growth and evolution. You evolve because of your desire and perseverance to become *more*. You seek positive changes that bring about personal growth when you are no longer willing to accept certain aspects of yourself as "good enough."

Your willingness to work at self-improvement is largely driven by an unremitting desire to feel authentic and whole. As you begin to implement even the most subtle changes, you feel an altruistic happiness. This positive feeling compels you to move forward along your journey of self-evolution.

Your capacity for self-evolution is limitless.

All that you require is the guidance of your intuitive self and the desire for self-actualization. Through self-evolution, you become *whole*.

DAILY PRACTICE: SELF-EVOLUTION

What characteristics hold you back from becoming who you want to be? What would you be willing to do to improve upon who you already are? Consider creating a list of attributes that you are willing to change and then develop several positive action steps for each change that you seek. Use your conscious awareness to bring attention to those moments where you have an opportunity to behave differently. Make the commitment to continue working on these self-improvements, even if the changes you seek come slowly.

The second universal purpose is to help others.

Pay attention to the number of opportunities that occur each day for helping another living being. You can choose to look with conscious awareness for chances to be helpful or you can ignore these purposeful moments. Helping others usually involves a simple gesture and it is never at the expense of your own well-being. Choosing to help, if practiced on a global scale, changes the way the world operates.

Notice what happens when you act with kindness, helping others when possible.

DAILY PRACTICE: HELPING OTHERS

The degree to which you help others goes far beyond what you might think possible. For example, passing your subway stop in order to accompany an ill tourist to the local city hospital may be the act of kindness that they remember with gratitude for years to come. Offering a kind word or a warm smile to the grocery cashier is an act of kindness that positively influences that person's outlook for the entire day.

The third universal purpose is to love unconditionally.

To love unconditionally means that you *are loving* in all of your actions and in how you treat yourself and others. You demonstrate unconditional love by choosing to respond with kindness, respect, and patience rather than judgment, intolerance, and criticism. You continue to act with the dignity of love, gentleness, and compassion even when others may be unable to do the same.

Daily Practice: Unconditional Love

What daily challenges could inspire you to practice unconditional love? Strive to live this universal purpose even when, for example: another driver passes you without warning, before cutting in front of you at the last minute; a server at a restaurant leaves you unattended for an extended period and then appears indignant when asked to take your order; a family member who behaves with an inappropriate level of anger and hostility in discussing a point of conflict with you. To love unconditionally—particularly in these moments—means to rise above whatever your instinctual reaction might be and instead to act with love and kindness. To practice unconditional love at particularly difficult moments requires conscious thought and self-control. To operate from a place of unconditional love suggests self-evolution.

To love unconditionally, to help others, and to practice self-evolution requires discipline, effort, and wisdom. These same qualities are what you practice inherently as you live your life's purpose.

CHAPTER FIVE

'Life' Lessons

*We evolve in consciousness and in spirit
through the mastery of life lessons.*

The situations and experiences that challenge us have the potential to teach valuable "life lessons." When we resist change—either by ignoring or denying our intuitive wisdom—we become mired in disparaging thoughts and feelings of hopelessness and despair.

We remain unable to resolve our situation until we are willing to look at it with consciousness.

All life lessons have the common purpose of helping us evolve. If we live consciously, we can look beyond our initial perception of any situation to find the essential lesson that lies beneath. With ingenious perfection, our life lessons teach us exactly what we need to learn at that particular time. True to form, a life lesson will continue to present itself until we "master" it. Recognize the life lessons inherent in the reoccurring challenges you face.

Mastering a life lesson means that you change your current situation by behaving differently.

You evolve and move in a direction that serves your higher purpose.

Simple, yet important, life lessons include *learning*:

patience; kindness; honesty; compassion; how to use "your voice;" how to create (and honour) healthy boundaries in your relationships; how to trust others (and yourself); forgiveness; and how to *live in your truth.*

All life lessons are interrelated. Think of them as beads that have been carefully strung on a thread. Each bead represents one of the quintessential lessons you have learned. Each one teaches you something of significant value—often building on what came before it.

When clients describe being immobilized by their current life situation, I encourage them to identify an unlearned life lesson as an opportunity for creating positive change.

Naomi is a good example of this. She is compassionate and kind and feels a great deal of empathy for others. One of the life lessons she continues to struggle with is learning how to set personal boundaries—to say "no"—without feeling bad about herself. Naomi believes that saying "no" to someone means that she is selfish. Because she has low self-esteem, she puts others' needs and demands before her own, in part so others will like her. Doing this, Naomi often ends up feeling anxious and depressed as she also feels people take advantage of her.

Recently, Naomi lent a large sum of money to her friend Terri. Four months have gone by without any mention from Terri of repayment. Not only does Naomi feel bad about bringing up the loan, but she also worries constantly about whether she will be repaid. Naomi has begun to feel as though she has made a big mistake and that Terri was simply using her.

Two months earlier, Naomi found herself driving a colleague home each night after work. What began as a kind gesture one evening during a storm quickly became an unspoken expectation on the part of her co-worker. Sheila began to wait for Naomi every night after work and would also ask her to run errands before being dropped off at home. Naomi admits feeling terrified when she thinks about discussing her feelings with Sheila. Even though she feels used, Naomi continues to comply with Sheila's unstated expectation. Naomi's biggest fear is that if she speaks her mind, Sheila will become angry and end their friendship.

In a separate example involving her sister, this same life lesson shows up again. Eva lives with Naomi but rarely contributes toward any of the groceries or living expenses. Eva has not worked for the past four years, living off of the money she made by selling her house. Whenever Naomi brings up the subject of paying rent or contributing to household expenses, Eva becomes defensive and starts to cry. Naomi feels as though her sister is taking advantage of her, and yet she can't bring herself to take a stand in order to put her own needs first.

Examining her current challenges as opportunities to learn life lessons, Naomi began to identify her needs as a priority. She practiced saying "no" to some requests that were made of her instead of placing others' needs before her own. Realizing that saying "no" didn't make her a selfish person, Naomi could begin to create healthy boundaries for the first time in her life.

Learning this valuable life lesson meant that Naomi could be kind and compassionate, and yet make choices that honoured her needs.

By recognizing your experiences as opportunities for learning, you become a force in shaping your destiny. When you master a life lesson, your old behaviour no longer exists. You evolve as a result of applying the knowledge and wisdom that your life lesson has taught you.

Judith recalled her experiences growing up with an older sister whom she described as aggressive, selfish, and controlling. As Judith began to replay her relationship with her older sister from the perspective of what life lessons she still needed to learn, she realized that she was finally addressing the emotional pain that she had carried for more than twenty-five years. Acknowledging that one of her life lessons was to learn how to *use her voice* was overwhelmingly freeing for Judith. In fact, this lesson turned up in many areas of her life.

By examining her sister's behaviour from a different perspective, Judith thought about what life lesson she might still learn. In no time, Judith found herself voicing her needs (rather than allowing herself to be bullied by her sister and others). For Judith, mastering this long-standing life lesson meant that she was free of feeling victimized by her sister.

Your particular life lessons are specific to you. They provide you with an opportunity to learn what you need in order to live your life's purpose.

Inherent in all life lessons are such fundamental qualities as:

- **Trust** in the natural process of life, in *karma* (what you reap *you will sow*); in receiving what it is that you need
- **Respect** of self, of others, of nature, and the environment
- **Honour,** being true to one's self and in what is right and best for you
- **Generosity** of spirit, of time, of kindness, and of money
- **Honesty**, being truthful and honourable in what you say and do

Carmen struggles with her mother's interference in her life. Her mother makes a point of telling her (a 44-year-old woman with her own two children) what to do. This includes anything from what kind of birthday gift to buy for her husband to what type of sheets would be best for her daughter's bed. Carmen tries politely to assert herself but generally feels smothered and henpecked. She wants to have a different kind of relationship with her mother and yet nothing she does seems to make a difference.

Daily Practice: Identifying My Life Lesson

Like Carmen, perhaps you tend to experience what feels like "the same old" frustrating conversations with a friend or loved one. Use the visualization exercise that follows to help you gain insight and confidence as you identify a life lesson.

Close your eyes and recall a familiar, albeit uncomfortable, scenario that continues to replay itself in your life. How do you typically react? How does your usual behaviour leave you feeling? What is the typical outcome?

Consider for a moment what life lesson may be integral to this recurring situation? How would you prefer to respond if it happens again? How would you feel behaving differently?

Now, imagine yourself in the near future. As you play through the beginning of this familiar scenario, imagine that you have the ability *to be different*. Pay attention to your new behaviours and to the positive outcome you created. See your new behaviours as the result of learning a particular life lesson. How do you feel at this moment as a result of being different?

By recording your answers, you identify what you need to do to achieve a different outcome in repeating situations. Your new behaviour is the life lesson that you need to master. (You may choose to identify your life lesson in a written statement). Being able to experience the *feeling* of what it would be like to operate differently, helps motivate and inspire you to learn this lesson.

Use this process to identify any other life lessons that may be presenting themselves to you.

As Carmen did this exercise, she envisioned a typical scenario. She imagined speaking on the phone with her mother, talking about what was going on in her life. Carmen's mother would almost always have a definite (and often narrow) viewpoint on how she should go about doing something. Carmen knew that if she chose to keep information to herself (to avoid her mother's unsolicited comments), it would typically backfire and her mother would be hurt and offended. Her mother would then criticize Carmen for shutting her out.

Using the visualization exercise, Carmen realized that the life lesson she needed to learn was self-confidence. Carmen realized that she had historically reinforced her mother's (bad) behaviour by always going to her for advice and input. As a result, Carmen never felt confident about making her own decisions, and would frequently look to her mother for validation.

Further discussion with Carmen revealed that she rarely made a decision without consulting someone.

Her life lesson—which continued to show up not only in her relationship with her mother but with her husband, her friends, and her co-workers—was to become confident in her own decision-making ability. As Carmen practiced the new behaviours she learned from this life lesson, we also began work on building healthy self-esteem. For the first time in her life, Carmen felt empowered. She felt that she was finally becoming the person she needed to be.

INNER HEALING

Healing is a deliberate and conscious endeavour. Inner healing is analogous to evolving psychologically, spiritually, and emotionally.

The process of healing the hurts and wounds of your past, allows you to become whole.

Healing enables you to live your life based on pure joy. It is a life lesson that is integral to living an authentic existence.

Inner healing cannot begin without conscious awareness. Through consciousness, you seek positive change and self-improvement. Through your desire to evolve, you acknowledge those aspects of your self that hold you back from being authentic (and happy). From here, you can create intentions to be as you would rather be. Out of your intention, comes positive action. In your desire to live authentically, you recognize the necessity to heal.

Inner healing requires that you examine areas of your life that continue to cause pain and sadness. Trust your intuitive wisdom for guidance on what is needed to release that suffering. Healing almost always requires forgiveness—of your self and of others.

What aspects of your inner self require healing? Answer the questions below as a way of figuring out how you can heal.

DAILY PRACTICE: SELF-HEALING

Each of these questions is designed to help you think about how you can begin your inner healing. Using a journal, record answers based on your intuitive wisdom. You may be surprised at what your unconscious mind reveals as you allow your heart to speak rather than your head. As you examine your life in greater detail, you may find that you already have some of the answers you need.

1. What aspects of myself do I deny or dislike? These *can* be physical attributes but remember to look at your personality and character traits, as well as habits and behaviours.
2. What past or present life events continue to be painful for me? Describe the specific situation(s). Identify your feelings in each situation.
3. What problems or conflicts seem to reoccur in my relationships with others?
4. What could I change that would allow me to be happier with myself?
5. What do *I need to do* to heal? Find a quiet place where you can easily hear your intuitive voice. Without judging the answer, do what you need to do to heal.

Inner healing sometimes involves resolving unfinished business from your family of origin. Without the tools for healing from these earlier experiences, you will undoubtedly spend most of your adult life re-living old hurts and wounds. Inner healing does not require you to be in contact with a person from your past who has hurt you. It may help you to obtain a greater understanding of the situation and of the causes involved, but inner healing is fundamentally self-directed. You decide what aspects of yourself you need to heal.

Section Three

CHAPTER SIX

From a Place of Spirit

*To operate from a place of spirit is to exude kindness
and compassion towards every living thing.*

Spirit is the energy or *life force* present in all living things. Your spirit (or inner self) evolves as an integral aspect of your being. To live from a place of spirit means that your thoughts and actions are motivated by kindness, compassion, and love. It means that you are able to share your self without any expectation of what you ought to receive in return.

When you choose to operate from *a place of spirit*, who you are becomes much larger than who you could ever imagine being. Just as a living tree grows in size and strength, its roots spreading deeper and deeper as it expands in magnitude, so does your capacity to share your self. As a tree produces incredible flowers, which in turn grow delicious fruit that others may feel nourished by, using your gifts as you live your life's purpose means that you too are able to nourish countless others.

Look for opportunities to share your spirit—your inner self—with others. Sharing your innate talents and gifts becomes not only what you do (your purpose), but also *who you are*.

Rejuvenating Your Spirit

By devoting time each day to soul work, you rejuvenate your spirit. By nourishing your spirit you feed your soul. Soul work strengthens the connection to your spirit— and your real purpose for being in this world at this time.

It allows you to create a place from which you are able to give freely of your self to others. It allows you to *feel joy*—not only as a result of your enjoyment of the activities that you choose to do, but because they provide you with a way of connecting with your inner self.

A simple way to define some of your favourite soul work activities is to spend a few moments considering all the things that bring you *joy*. Your list might include such simple luxuries as: hot baths, playing with your children, relaxing in your favourite chair, enjoying a cup of coffee while you read the Sunday paper, laughing, leisurely motorcycle rides through the country, or walking in the park with your dog. All of the things that bring you joy also deepen your connection to your inner self and to the universe at large.

The things you most love to do *nourish your soul*. When you feel nourished and content it is easier to feel gratitude for the richness and fullness of life. In nourishing your soul, you feel connected with your inner self. When you are aware of your spirit, it is easy to experience pure joy.

Soul work activities encourage your *creative* energy. They also create physical and mental clarity. Activities that feed your soul enable you to feel grounded and centred. You feel alive and vital and, at the same time, experience a sense of inner calm and peace. From this place you are more easily able to share your gifts.

Think for a moment about the soul work you do now. What do you do for your self that brings you joy and gives you a sense of fulfillment? What would life be like if you made a conscious effort to begin every day with soul work? When you make it a regular practice to do soul work you easily notice when a few days have gone by without your paying any attention to your inner self. You feel out of balance, as if something fundamentally important to your well-being is missing.

Making soul work activities a priority allows you to share your self with others. You share your self in simple yet profound ways. You're more likely to offer a kind word or a smile to a stranger or to help a loved one through a difficult situation. Soul work allows you to carry out your life's purpose. To live from a place of spirit is your greatest accomplishment and the resulting inner contentment perpetuates your desire to continue doing so.

Think for a moment of what would happen if every one of us were taught to practice *soul work*. What would we accomplish as a community, a country—or a planet—if everyone operated from a place of spirit?

DAILY PRACTICE: SOUL WORK ACTIVITIES

The next time you're doing something that you enjoy, pay attention to how you feel in that moment.

Allow yourself to simply be present with what you're doing, giving that particular activity your full attention.

Notice how this activity *makes you feel* and *where in your body* you feel this sensation, particularly in terms of your connection to your inner self.

Establish the connection between an activity you enjoy and how you experience it in your body. This is a helpful way to remind you of the benefit of engaging in regular soul* work.

When you are caught up in a state of constant activity, it is easy to forget about nourishing your soul. For most people, keeping busy is a way of life. We spend an enormous part of our lives focused on our accomplishments at work, our involvement in activities, and our relationships with others. We have commitments and responsibilities to our children, spouse or

---

* Your soul is by definition eternal and usually believed to preexist the body.

significant other, friends, extended family, and our job. Often our devotion to things outside of our self becomes the primary focus of our attention.

It's important to remember that your ability to give *freely* of your self to others starts with your ability to nourish your own self. Without being able to nourish your inner self, you operate from a place of obligation and duty, rather than free will. Others notice your subtle but growing bitterness or resentment, and ultimately, you lose touch with the feelings that might naturally have arisen if you were operating out of a place of intention and love. When your soul is neglected, you feel less connected within, and as a result, lack control over your life.

With attention to your spirit and regular practice of soul work, you nourish your inner self. You create daily quiet time for introspection, reflection, and meditation, becoming far more equipped to make the best choices in your life. You become skilled at recognizing when you begin to feel *drained* of your resources. Knowing that you need to stop and replenish your inner self (even just taking a few deep breaths in order to return to the present moment), allows you to feel in control of your life.

WITHOUT EGO

Ego, Latin for "I", is often associated with the word "egocentric"—or the need to satisfy your pride and your sense of self-importance. Ego is a human quality, driven by our momentary need to prove our worth. Your ego creates your internal dialogue ("the story you convince yourself is true"). Without consciousness, your ego seems to be an automatic response, but it is actually both instinctive and learned. You develop your ego out of fear of judgment, insecurity, and low self-esteem, and as it is a defence mechanism—it comes out of a perceived need to defend yourself when you feel threatened.

When you operate from a place of ego, you judge others, determining that they are somehow inferior to you. You resort to using your ego to feel a (false) sense of security or comfort about your self and your life. Your ego becomes a way for you to temporarily feel better about yourself.

Operating out of ego keeps you in a place of satisfying your own wants first, often at the expense of others. Your sense of self is compromised because you are not living in your truth. You are concerned with your pride and are reluctant to allow others to see your vulnerabilities. Your exchanges with other people are cursory and artificial since it is impossible to connect with others on any level of authenticity. Others feel the need to defend themselves and operate out of ego also. Ego begets ego. Ego keeps you disconnected from your inner self.

Living in your ego can help you avoid going within to address the void or emptiness you feel. It can be tempting to allow your ego to define you and consequently, you spend a lot more time reinforcing your ego as well as hiding behind it. Eventually, your ego ends up consuming you. Your daily choices and actions become a direct result of ego rather than love, compassion, and authenticity.

Think of authenticity as "living in your truth." With authenticity, the person others see is who you actually are. You don't need to hide behind walls of ego or shame because your authenticity means that you are comfortable enough with yourself to be able to show your self to the rest of the world. When you choose authenticity, you attract others who are also authentic. You feel empowered because who you are is who you allow others to see.

Forgiveness, compassion, and acceptance are three qualities that support your ability to live from a place of spirit. Notice how easy it becomes to practice these with conscious awareness.

ACCEPTANCE

We say that we accept others for who they are, even when we continue to make negative judgments about them. We behave outwardly as though we accept who we are, while secretly we loathe and reject aspects of our self. We tell others that we accept what they say, and quietly doubt or disregard it. Every day we hear people complaining about some aspect of their lives, wishing that it were different. All of this would suggest that most of us haven't begun to master the art of acceptance, in fact, we are far from it.

Acceptance and understanding are highly interdependent.

By attempting to understand others' differences, you can more easily accept who they are.

You are far less likely to make wrong assumptions or negative judgments when you understand someone's beliefs, values, and situation. With greater understanding comes the ability to accept and to offer compassion.

Acceptance means that you can allow each living being to be who and what they are in this moment.

While you might like someone to be different—more patient, more intelligent, less serious, happier, a better listener—you cannot create those changes. While the person may change at some point in the future, acceptance means that you allow them to be who they are.

Practicing acceptance wholeheartedly means that you no longer blame others for what you see as their flaws. Instead, who they are is enough. While you may not always agree with the way others behave or choose to live their lives, you can accept that they have chosen a different path than you and that you can't begin to judge their choices without living as them. When you give up trying to change someone and instead accept them for who they are (appreciating the fact that they may be all that they can be at that moment), you free up a significant amount of time and energy to be able to share of your self.

When you can't accept yourself fully, the world can be a frightening place. Without self-acceptance, you are left feeling inadequate and "not good enough." You are far too influenced and affected by what others say and do. Without self-acceptance, you can never be happy (enough) with yourself.

DAILY PRACTICE: DEVELOPING ACCEPTANCE

Create an exhaustive list of the things that allow you to feel adequate. Create a second list, describing the ways in which you accept yourself—as you are.

You begin to accept yourself by reminding yourself of all that already makes you feel adequate and that you accept unconditionally. Continue to add to your lists over time.

Use the following sentence stem exercise to draw out other examples from your life as a means of reinforcing and expanding your acceptance of self. Complete each of the sentence stems below with *at least* six endings. Repeat this exercise each day for at least one week before reviewing your answers.

I can accept ....

I am adequate because........

On some level, we all struggle with self-acceptance. We strive to achieve the goals that govern how we define our success. We envision how we would like to look, feel, be, and do and what we would like to have in our lives. And yet, in the same breath, we remain doubtful, self-critical, anxious, and envious. All of this would suggest that we have not attained self-acceptance. Being able to fully embrace all of what we are requires ongoing effort, gratitude, and above all, self-love.

Self-acceptance is about being happy with who you are in this moment. It means feeling comfortable in your own skin and with where you currently are in your self-evolution. You need to remember that you don't define *self* by what you want to become, but rather by who you are at this moment. Practicing self-acceptance is fundamental to taking responsibility for your own happiness. Accepting your self (including your positive attributes *and* your self-identified flaws) makes it far easier to accept others. To be accepting of your self means that you are willing to take a close look at who you currently are (even as you may be working on self-improvement) and be okay with that. It's a lot easier to accept who you are if you are conscious of all of your personal strengths, achievements, and abilities.

COMPASSION

Compassion is elicited out of acts of kindness, caring, and generosity. It brings about selfless acts of helping others.

Compassion requires that you feel a sense of connection to another—even if it is only for a moment, and directed toward a complete stranger. You connect most easily through empathy. When you attempt to step into another person's shoes and imagine what it must be like to experience their life (at that particular moment), you feel empathy. The experience of empathy softens your perception toward other human beings. It makes compassion possible.

When you practice compassion, others feel comforted because you have made an effort to understand them better, rather than to pass judgment. The objective in eliciting compassion is for you to step outside of your *biased* way of thinking long enough to acknowledge that to accept others' differences requires an understanding of those differences. Understanding comes from asking thoughtful questions and being open to embrace difference.

Daily Practice: Developing Compassion

In any situation where your intention is to become compassionate, ask yourself:

1. How would *I* feel if I were in this situation?
2. How would I want to be treated if I were this person?
3. What will help me to understand this person's behaviour?
4. How do I want to be reacting right now?
5. How can I show kindness and caring?
6. What life lesson might I need to learn from this situation?

Compassion allows you to honour and respect others. You see others with love and kindness, which in turn affects the way you treat them. With acceptance and compassion, you are able to forgive.

FORGIVENESS

Think of forgiveness as a *fundamental way of being in the world*—as something that you choose to do on a *daily basis*. Practicing forgiveness allows you to operate from a place of spirit. Offering forgiveness means that you no longer need to be caught up in the negative inner dialogue that comes with judging others as "wrong," "inappropriate" or "hurtful." Being forgiving (quietly and inwardly), allows you to move forward rather than be weighed down in all of the critical self-talk and dark feelings that go together with your negative perception of a situation.

For example, what if your initial instinct were to offer forgiveness to the speeding driver who has just cut you off in traffic? What if you automatically extended forgiveness to someone who has just made a comment that hurt your feelings? Perhaps forgiveness could be what you immediately offer your partner when he or she is abrupt or impatient. Think about how you can extend forgiveness in all of the life events that happen on a daily basis. Notice how important forgiveness is in all of your relationships.

The word of forgiveness tends to be so overused it has become meaningless. As a result, we give it lip service, although in truth, it is elusive. Even when you *decide* to forgive someone, it's not uncommon to feel a pang of resentment, hurt, or anger the moment you think back to the specific incident in question. This unfinished business resonates because forgiveness is not always easy to *complete*. You can intellectually make the decision to forgive someone, but still hold on to the pain, hurt, or anger that you initially felt. If you hold on to hurtful emotions, you cannot complete the intention of forgiveness.

Daily Practice: Developing Forgiveness

You forgive when you can develop compassion and acceptance toward another being. You may intend to forgive, but it isn't until you are able to let go of how you believe you *ought* to have been treated and any anger and hurt that you feel, and instead look for a way of accepting with compassion what was.

Recognize that the individual you want to forgive was doing their best given their limitations. Rather than judge those limitations, allow yourself to feel empathy. You begin by allowing yourself to forgive their actions—their humanness—as they, like you, are not perfect. With forgiveness of someone's actions, you can then work on forgiving the individual.

Sometimes, to forgive someone *completely* may take far longer than you might expect—particularly if you have a longstanding history of unresolved wounds (as in a parent/child relationship). Seek a greater understanding of the individual's circumstances at that time, either with their help or by attempting to view the past situation from the perspective of the limited knowledge or ability they may have had. Often, hearing an apology (even years later) can help make it easier to let go and forgive.

Forgiveness also needs to be directed inwardly. To forgive yourself, let go of your self-critical thoughts to allow for acceptance and healing. Acknowledge what it is specifically that you find fault with. Then, ask your inner self what is required to release self-blame.

Remember that forgiving yourself is easier when you have healthy self-esteem. When you dislike or devalue yourself, you focus on any behaviours that highlight your imperfections. These become further evidence supporting your belief that you are flawed or not good enough rather than simply mistakes.

Forgiveness needs to be an ever-present part of your life. It is through forgiveness and acceptance rather than self-criticism that you can make important changes to who you are. Forgiveness of yourself and others enables you to heal. You can't possibly live in a place of spirit when you feel resentful and hurt.

Your Dark Side

You are vulnerable to your dark side at moments when you are disconnected from your inner self (your spirit). Your dark side is observed as a lack of self-control, and originates out of the negative and unfounded stories (your inner dialogue) you convince yourself are true. You become mired in ego and lack of self-awareness. The resulting unrealistic expectations and biased frame of reference evoke a combination of such emotions as anger, hostility, hurt, jealousy, and sadness. As a result, you behave in a manner that does not reflect your true self.

To deny or hide this imperfect part of yourself doesn't prevent your dark side from revealing itself. Your dark side is the part of you that gets in the way of your being who you have the potential to be. It is when you act out of your dark side that you feel remorseful for your actions.

Much of the time, your dark side is short-lived. After losing control of your temper and shouting angrily at your child you may reflect for the next few minutes, feeling bad for your reaction. When you justify your impatience and anger by telling yourself that your behaviour was appropriate and necessary, you prolong the time you spend in your dark side. Giving in to your dark side keeps you from experiencing authentic happiness. Because your inner self is in conflict, you are not able to share yourself with genuine love and compassion. In your dark side, you remain hostage to your ego. When you decide to acknowledge it, your dark side is an obvious reminder of the work you still need to do on yourself.

Just like each moment of your life requires a new breath, each moment also requires a conscious choice to conduct yourself from a place of spirit. As you evolve it becomes easier to choose how you will be in each moment. Each new moment carries with it a new set of possibilities—all within your reach. As evolved as you become in this lifetime, you will always need to remain fully conscious of how you choose to be in each moment.

Choosing to live from a place of spirit rather than from your dark side means paying greater attention to your own needs. Invest time each day in renewing and rebuilding your spirit (your inner self). Such qualities as compassion, love, empathy, understanding, patience, and kindness are only some examples of what you need to attend to. When you commit to self-discovery and self-reflection you honour your need to evolve. You acknowledge that there is continued learning and growth that opens your eyes to a better way of being in your life. Being committed to personal introspection and self-honesty rejuvenates your spirit, allowing you to effectively handle everyday situations in a way that reflects your highest self.

With awareness of your dark side, you become

skilled at anticipating those moments when you are vulnerable to it. You are also quick to recognize those occasions when you fall prey to moments of darkness. This awareness brings immediate attention to your thoughts, feelings, and behaviours. From here, you can make consciously inspired decisions to operate instead from a place of spirit.

Take a moment to answer the questions that follow. Your responses will help you identify your dark side as well as understand what causes you to get stuck there.

Daily Practice: Identifying My Dark Side

1. How would I characterize my *dark side*? What does it look like to someone observing me? (List as many mannerisms, traits, and behaviours that define your dark side as possible.)

2. What are some of the early warning signs that let me know that I am moving into my dark side? What are my inner thoughts? Is there a pattern that I can identify?

3. What are some of my biggest *regrets* from living in my dark side? (What have I said or done that made me feel remorseful?)

Reflect on previous moments when you were in your dark side. Imagine yourself in a similar situation in the future operating instead from a place of spirit. Visualise how differently you would behave. Hold this positive image in your mind for a few moments to anchor the feelings.

If you have been spending too much time in your dark side, perhaps you have not been doing enough to renew and rejuvenate your inner self. If it is left unattended long enough, inner conflict and turmoil begin to take up a large part of your daily existence.

In fact, one thing I consistently notice in my clients is that they have long stopped paying attention to their inner needs and to renewing their spirit. They have stopped doing what feeds their soul, making it virtually impossible to feel connected within. Ultimately they forget, or (in some cases), have never learned how to create authentic happiness. One of the inherent benefits to therapy is having someone direct you to stop what you *have been* doing and to become fully conscious in what you *are* doing. Therapy challenges you to examine your inauthentic behaviour, and to make positive changes that will enable you to live in your truth.

Rejuvenating your spirit with soul work includes carving out quiet time to reflect, meditate and imagine. When you pay attention to the needs of your inner self, you are more likely to fulfill these since you make your self a priority. As a result, you are less likely to spend time in your dark side.

CHAPTER SEVEN

Daily Life Practice

*Creating new ways of being requires you to practice
daily life habits.*

Daily guiding principles helps you to remember that, above all else, it is your *intention to become more* that creates everything else. Through self-awareness you access inner wisdom. You begin to trust your instincts to guide you as you strive to make changes that will allow you to become more.

The inspiration for positive change begins with consciousness. Remember to be patient. Patience and perseverance in the face of challenging old habits is the key to creating lasting changes. Your personal growth, up to and including the ultimate fulfillment of your life's purpose, depends largely on the purposeful actions you take each day.

Below are three practices that will support the new ways of being that you have initiated. Use each of these as guiding principles in living purposefully.

INTENTION

Intention predicates action. Creating intentions as part of your daily practice for how you want to be and for living your life, means that you are far more likely to achieve your destiny.

Out of self-awareness and self-knowledge comes the *intention* to evolve—to live a more meaningful life. Conscious intention means that you have identified the changes that you desire. Every time you create an intention, whether you realize it or not, your unconscious mind begins to move toward that desire.

Our conscious intention is our free will. It's like saying to the universe: "I would like this to happen. I would like to create this in my life." Having clear intention is the key to making something a reality. Intention precedes action and provides you with a focus for what it is that you want to create.

Without intention, you move through life as a recipient of what happens. While I'm not suggesting that you can control every life circumstance, you *can* affect much by way of having a particular intention (thought, picture, or idea) of what you want to create. You can create intentions for everything including moments of simply being fully present.

Living with intention means that you have a plan and purpose for your life.

It also means regularly reviewing the direction your life is moving in to reassess whether that direction is still the best one for you. You live with intention by actively creating and acting on goals and life objectives. By breaking your larger plans into goals (short-, medium-, and long-term), you can formulate action steps. Action steps provide a direction or focus—essentially a daily intention—for how you want to live. Achieving your major life goals, come directly out of *conscious* daily intentions—your steps of action toward those goals.

You can create an intention for just about anything: what you want to accomplish at work on any particular day; exploring what courses are offered in a particular college program that interests you; or strengthening your relationship with your partner by spending quality time in honest conversation. Because your thoughts precede your behaviours, it makes sense that what you do follows from what you most think about. In other words,

how you live your life comes largely from how you think about living it.

Remember that your intentions need to be specific. You must have clear and distinct thoughts for what you want to create. Wavering or doubtful thoughts mean your intentions are not clear. As a result, your actions are more likely to be in line with those inner doubts or fears and not with what you really want.

Daily Practice: Creating Intentions

Some suggestions for using intention as a daily practice:

- Think of one or two intentions for yourself at the start of your day.
- Frame your intentions as positives: i.e. "I want to....", "I am ...", "I will be...."
- Create intentions for what you need as well as ones that involve your interactions with others. e.g. "I need to feel relaxed." / "I need to be patient with others."

Listen to your intuitive self when you create intentions for a specific day. Sometimes your initial thought will concern an intention to feel loved or to have a sense of peacefulness. These are general intentions and yet they are very useful as guidelines for how you can choose to be on that particular day.

Keep your intentions in the forefront of your mind. Record them where you can be reminded of them throughout the day. Your intentions will help you to seek out what it is that you are looking for. At the end of each day, recall your intentions and look for evidence that they were met in some way. This will also help strengthen your belief in their ability to work for you.

Once you have created the intentions for what you want for yourself, the daunting task is: How will you go about making these changes possible? It is one thing to recognize how you would like to be, but it is quite another thing to be able to change successfully. *Knowing how* you could behave differently—and how you would measure your progress for making those desired changes—is the tricky part.

Perhaps you would like to be able to trust the people closest to you. You recognize the difficulty you have had in doing this, given your earlier life experiences. Being consciously aware of your actions in relationships with others reminds you that you tend to keep others at a safe distance, never really letting your guard down. The end result is that you don't feel especially close to the people who are important to you. You have never allowed yourself to trust others.

Or, maybe you recognize that you tend to rely on others for your happiness rather than creating it for yourself. You recognize that when you blame others for what is not right in your life, you continue to feel helpless and victimized and, incidentally, nothing ever changes. Through conscious awareness, you realize that your happiness is ultimately up to you. You can decide that it's time you began taking responsibility for what is not right in your life and move toward changing it.

Perhaps you recognize the need to be kinder and more accepting of others. In those moments where you would typically find yourself becoming impatient, you can begin to pay attention to your inner thoughts. In doing so, you will realize that your behaviours are a direct result of your unrealistically high expectations of others.

Through conscious intention, you are able to experience greater meaning and purpose in all that you do. By being self-aware and self-responsible, you can be open and willing to take a close look at all of your qualities – including those that you might struggle with.

At the end of the day, change ultimately comes from your commitment to change. You can't begin to make any changes without taking your blindfold off. You need to see things as they really are—to shine a huge flashlight on your flaws, your imperfections, and your ego—highlighting to yourself what you might previously have chosen to ignore. It's like saying, "Wow. I really need to change this about myself in order to be a ... better, kinder, more loving... person!"

Being aware of your behaviours—particularly those behaviours that you may be less proud of—is an important step toward changing them. The mere fact that you are aware of your tendency to be critical or judgmental of others, for example, is a *huge* step. Out of this willingness to see yourself for who you are, comes choice. You no longer go through life unaware of your self. You now have choice for how you want to be.

Having the conscious intention to want more from your life means that you are willing to look at each new challenge as an opportunity to learn valuable information about yourself, to grow and evolve. It's as if the universe is supporting your desire by saying, "This is an important life lesson that you will need to learn."

Finally, it's important to remember that change—particularly change that involves the self—occurs relatively slowly. Sometimes you will "slip up"—reverting to old habits and old ways of being. You will feel old behaviours being triggered by those closest to you. In fact, you will still have "regretful moments" where you find yourself acting in exactly the way that you have spent months working so hard to change. And yet, that is part of the process for creating the long-lasting changes you are looking for. There is purpose to feeling displeased, embarrassed, and ashamed of your actions even as you are attempting to change them, in order to be reminded of how important it remains to keep working at them.

If you continue to go through life without being conscious of your actions—living in denial or blaming others for your shortcomings—then you can never be fully responsible for your self and your behaviour. Without self-responsibility, you will not see any point to changing. You will repeat the same patterns, act out in the same ways, and feel the same unpleasant emotions.

The truth is that you have a great deal of *control* over how your life unfolds. You have control over your free will up to the moment you die. What you may not realize is that your intentions are largely controlled by your day-to-day thoughts—as is the free will you use to choose how you want to live your life.

Because of your conscious intention to live your life with full awareness—with eyes wide open—you begin to make conscious choices toward the specific outcomes that you want to create. You live your life with the knowledge that you will create what it is that you think most about. Knowing this gives you the capacity to create positive intentions for the goals you want to achieve, and for the unlimited possibilities of your life.

INFINITE LEARNING

Your second daily practice is the notion of infinite learning. Remember that one of your most valuable gifts is your ability to evolve. You evolve by being willing to take a close look at your self.

Your evolution takes place because of your willingness to learn and to integrate those lessons into your life.

If you view every interaction, circumstance, and situation as an opportunity to learn something, then you will. Being open to what you might learn from another is extremely valuable. As soon as you open yourself to the possibility that others can always teach you something, you become more attentive and conscious to all of your experiences. You discover that you learn exactly what you need at any given time.

There are always individuals who can teach you valuable lessons about ways of being. Pay close attention. Observe the actions of everyone. Hear them speak about how they live *their* lives. Ask questions. If you remain open to what you can learn from others, you will always create opportunities for infinite learning.

Remember that much of what you can learn from others is unsolicited. Inspiring people remind you that it *is* possible to live a meaningful life. And yet, people who live their life in a way that promotes chaos and exemplifies a lack of consciousness teach you valuable lessons as well. These people remind you of what life is like when you choose (either directly or indirectly) to search outside of yourself for happiness; they remind you of how temporary the feeling is when you attempt to make yourself feel better by seeking power or control over another. Even the negative behaviours you witness serve to help you by reminding you of what you choose to not be.

By being open to the information and knowledge that comes into your life on a daily basis, you grow and evolve. Look at casual conversations and daily exchanges with others as possibilities for learning. Listen for new ways of thinking and being in the world. Be open to new experiences and ways of understanding. All of this promotes self-discovery, evolution, and inner wisdom.

Daily Practice: Infinite Learning

Some suggestions for using infinite learning as a daily practice:

- After a conversation with a friend, loved one, or stranger get into the habit of asking yourself: "What can I learn from this?" or "What can this person teach me?"
- As you walk or drive down a familiar street, look for something new that you have never seen before. Observe others. Notice what they are teaching you through your simply observing them.
- When you are sharing your self with family or friends, listen carefully to what they have to say, even if you don't always agree. Learn about how they live their lives through what they share with you. Without judging them, be conscious of what you can learn from them.

As you remain open to infinite learning, it's equally important to spend time reflecting on your own inner thoughts and behaviours. By being conscious of how others receive you and how you share who you are, you continue to develop your core self. Without holding a mirror up to your self, you can never learn or grow. To see your dark side with open eyes is far more powerful than to have anyone else show it to you. It's only through seeing yourself as honestly as possible that you can learn infinitely.

COMMITMENT

The practice of commitment as a third daily life practice is fundamental to maintaining any long-term change. Your commitment to adopt activities that cultivate positive change, and to see those changes through, enhances your self-confidence about what is possible. Remaining committed to the process of finding what you are seeking means staying focused on the end you have in mind. Maintaining your commitment to the changes you seek means that you will ultimately achieve these. As a daily life practice, commitment will ensure that you will continue to honour your goals: to live consciously, to learn the life lessons that are presented to you, and to use the gifts that help you live your life's purpose.

With commitment, you find opportunities to test new ways of being. Always seek to become more.

Daily Practice: Self-Commitment

Some suggestions for using commitment as a daily practice:

- Commitment relies on discipline. You may go through periods in which you wane in your commitment to make a particular change. Know that even small steps toward what you want to achieve mean that you are moving in the right direction. Your commitment will grow stronger after you have seen some of what is possible from your efforts. Get started even if your commitment level isn't one-hundred per cent just yet.
- Make commitments to yourself. As much as you might like to change because of another person, your commitment will be easier to achieve if it is something that you truly want to do for yourself.
- Allow yourself to dream a little. Don't be afraid to make a long-term commitment that you know will take time. Once you get started you will be surprised at how much momentum carries you forward.
- Continue to remind yourself of your commitments to yourself. Be prepared to motivate yourself from time to time. Keep your commitments written down where you can reflect on them often.

See everyday challenges as opportunities to practice (and eventually master) new behaviours. Be patient as you make the changes that you have identified for yourself. Having the intention to become different, and seeing opportunities as infinite sources of learning, means that *you will* continue to move in the direction of your ultimate life's purpose. Maintaining your commitment to the journey into your self ensures that you will achieve this.

Afterword

If you are listening to your inner voice, sometimes the reason *why* you need to do something isn't as important as the *knowing* that you *need* to do it. This inner knowing was a large part of how this book came to be: I simply felt a powerful need to write it.

In life, you will hear that inner voice directing you at times. Listen to it. Your inner voice has a way of guiding you in just the right direction, if you allow it.

Regardless of where you are on your personal journey—be on it. Do something to move towards becoming "more" in this lifetime. Life is too short to exist without having a purpose for why you are here.

Wishing you love and joy always,

Dorothy Ratusny

SELECTED BIBLIOGRAPHY

Branden, Nathaniel. *The Psychology of Self-Esteem.* New York: Bantam Books, 1969.

Branden, Nathaniel. *How To Raise Your Self-Esteem.* New York: Bantam Books, 1987.

Chopra, Deepak. *How to Know God: The Soul's Journey into the Mystery of Mysteries.* New York: Three Rivers Press, 2000.

Greenberger, Dennis and Christine Padesky. *Mind Over Mood: A Cognitive Therapy Treatment Manual for Clients.* New York: The Guilford Press, 1995.

His Holiness the Dalai Lama and Howard C. Cutler, M.D. *The Art of Happiness.* New York: Riverhead Books, 1998.

Lama Surya Das. *Awakening to the Sacred: Creating a Personal Spiritual Life.* New York: Broadway Books, 1999.

Lama Surya Das. *Awakening the Buddha Within: Tibetan wisdom for the western world.* London: Bantam Books, 1997.

Levoy, Gregg. *Callings: Finding and Following an Authentic Life.* New York: Three Rivers Press, 1997.

Ratusny, Dorothy. *The Purpose of Love: A guidebook for defining and cultivating your most significant relationship*. Toronto: Insomniac Press, 2007.

Sturgess, Stephen. *The Yoga Book: A practical and spiritual guide to self-realization.* London: Watkins Publishing, 2002.

Tolle, Eckhart. *The Power of Now.* Vancouver: Namaste Publishing Inc., 1997.

Van Praagh, James. *Healing Grief: Reclaiming Life After Any Loss.* New York: New American Library, 2000.

Van Praagh, James. *Talking to Heaven: A Medium's Message of Life After Death.* New York: Dutton, 1997.

ABOUT THE AUTHOR

Dorothy Ratusny is a psychotherapist specializing in Cognitive Therapy. She works with adolescents, adults, and couples in her private practice in Toronto, Canada, and via telephone and the Internet with clients across the country.

She is the author of *The Purpose of Love: A guidebook for defining and cultivating your most significant relationship* (Insomniac Press, 2007).

As a consultant for numerous corporations, Dorothy facilitates performance-based strategies and solutions in order to improve workplace communication and trust, and to strengthen relationships among both management and employees. In addition, she leads personalized corporate training programs and speaks on a wide range of topics to various professional groups and organizations.

Dorothy has written feature articles for several national publications, including *The Globe and Mail, Elle.ca, FAZE teen*, and *HEART Business Journal*. She has made numerous radio and television guest appearances including hosting the 13-week television documentary series, "Love Is Not Enough" featured on the *Life Network*. The series followed the unfolding drama of four couples as they worked to overcome unresolved issues and improve their relationships. She also was the co-host of *Womyn's Word* on CHRY 105.5 FM Radio in Toronto.

You may visit her website at: *www.dorothyratusny.com*.